RETRO CRICKET

Retro CRICKET

Ian Collis

NEW HOLLAND

Introduction

Like many youngsters who were born of the 1950s in the post-war 'baby-boomer' era, I was always surrounded by sport. If we weren't listening to their deeds on radio, watching them on television on a flickering, black and white screen or reading about them in the newspaper, we were trying to emulate our heroes on weekends on suburban cricket fields or down at the local park.

My father Joseph loved sport and this passion definitely rubbed off on me. Talk around the dinner table was never too far away from what was happening on the various sporting fields. I was to find this love of all things sport never leaves you and shapes your life. In fact, I walked away from a successful career in accounting in 1995 to pursue a career in sport statistics. As head of statistics at Fox Sports, my fulltime career is also my hobby as well as my passion.

As both a sports lover and an historian, I have always searched for stories and images from our past, be it our way of life, our culture or our pastimes. I have been searching for those special moments now for over 30 years, forever looking for that one 'shot' that captured a unique sporting moment, historical event or cultural milestone.

For the cricket enthusiast of bygone eras, watching the game on television – with super slow motion replays of every controversial incident or any of the other technology that is available today – was a distant dream in the future. If you wanted to watch a game of international cricket you went to the ground, or if that was not possible, listened to it on the radio or read about it in the newspapers the following day. In this regard, the sports photographer was all-important. He had to try and capture the controversy, the winning shot, an individual milestone and even the mood of the crowd to tell the story of the day. Many photographers, their names now lost in history, took wonderfully historic photos that never saw the light of day.

Many of these images have been lost for decades, collecting dust in corners of newspaper or publishing libraries or zealously collected and guarded by memorabilia hunters and sports lovers

Left: Sir Donald Bradman, the Australian Test captain, is everybody's hero in Australia. He is being surrounded by mostly women spectators as he went out to bat to resume his century innings for an Australian XI against the MCC in 1946 at the MCG.

Previous spread: The MCC and an Australian XI during play at the Melbourne Cricket Ground on 21 November 1946. Arthur Morris who had played himself into the Test team with some brilliant batting, has thrown himself full length in the slips to try to take a difficult chance offered by English batsman Len Hutton. His partner Cyril Washbrook is at the other end, Fred Freer is the bowler, Ron Saggers the wicket-keeper and Keith Miller the fieldsman with arms upraised. The chance was not taken when Hutton was 17 and he would go on to score an excellent 71.

alike. Through years of searching and building networks with other collectors, I have managed to locate many 'gems' that, when placed together in chronological order, tell a wonderful story of cricket and cricketers through the 'retro years' from the late 1940s to the 1970s. My search started in Australia, then onto England and finally to wherever cricket was played. I have been lucky enough to meet many interesting cricket lovers who have cherished these photos over the years, with some handed down from father to son and kept in personal collections for decades.

Together in this book, they tell a unique story. *Retro Cricket* traces the game from the mid-1940s as the world was free of the horrors of war through to the 1970s. For me these years were the golden era of sport, and especially so, for cricket. Before the 'Revolution of '77', cricket was a very different game … there were few one-day internationals, sparse advertising on the perimeters of grounds and certainly no coloured clothing with sponsor logos. Cricket was a game played by gentlemen, barely semi-professional, and the 'Test Match' was the ultimate contest. And the ultimate prize was the 'Ashes' trophy—a small terracotta urn holding the ashes of a burnt cricket bail—which has been the source of Anglo-Australian sporting endeavour for more than a hundred years.

Through the eyes of the game's photographers, that era comes to life again … cricketers ducking from bombs falling in London during WWII; Sir Donald Bradman batting at the end of his amazing career; Lindsay Hassett guiding Australia's fortunes in the post-Bradman era; the rise of the West Indies as a cricketing force; various 'Ashes' series as the fortunes of England and Australia ebbed and flowed during the different decades; the great South Africa teams of the 1950s and '60s, before their government's apartheid policies robbed a generation of Test cricketers their turn on the world stage; the pulsating Australia v West Indies series of 1960-61, including the first tied Test match; and the fledgling Pakistan, India and New Zealand teams as world cricket continued to prosper.

This book is presented in four main chapters devoted to each decade from the 1940s through to the 1970s. Each section showcases the leading players and matches in that decade. The first introductory chapter covers the era immediately after World War II. The highlight of the 1940s was Don Bradman's 'Invincibles' on their tour to England in 1948, some would rightly argue, Australia's greatest ever team … Bradman, Barnes, Morris, Miller, Brown, Hassett, Lindwall and Johnston to name a few.

The 1950s witnessed a new wave of cricketing greats … the three 'Ws' of Walcott, Weekes and Worrell of the West Indies; the wonderful England teams that included wicket-keeper Godfrey Evans, bowlers Trueman, Tyson and Laker, and batsmen Edrich, Cowdrey and May; and finally the rise of South Africa as a cricket powerhouse.

The 1960s is represented by a very extensive chapter in this book. When the West Indies toured Australia in the summer of 1960-61, the whole cricket world changed. The sheer abundance of talent, together with the excitement and controversy of each Test match played in a spirit of great sportsmanship reinvigorated the game. The two best teams in the world, led by two brilliant captains in Frank Worrell and Richie Benaud, showcased such stars as Garry Sobers, Lance Gibbs, Wes Hall, Rohan Kanhai, Norm O'Neill, Bobby Simpson and Alan Davidson.

The decade produced a veritable production line of stars, many of which are featured in this book. South Africa had the Pollock brothers, Peter and Graeme, Eddie Barlow, Trevor Goddard, Mike Proctor, Ali Bacher and Denis Lindsay. England's great fast-bowler Freddie Trueman surpassed 300 wickets; teammate Derek Underwood spun his magic on numerous occasions on wickets that suited, firebrand John Snow was a constant thorn for top-order batsmen around the world and England's batsmen Edrich, Boycott, Cowdrey and Barrington piled on the runs. Of the other leading countries, New Zealand continued to improve with talented players such as Bevan Congdon, Jim Reid, Bert Sutcliffe, Graham Dowling, Barry Sinclair; Pakistan produced Hanif Mohammed, Saeed Ahmed and Intikhab Alam, while India had the talents of the Nawab of Pataudi, Sunil Gavaskar, F.M. Engineer and E.A. Prasanna.

The final chapter, the 1970s, saw the game of cricket reach the crossroads. Cricket officialdom, dismayed by players' remuneration demands, set the seeds for a cricket revolution. In a tumultuous decade, the mighty South African side were barred from world cricket; Ray Illingworth's England team were at their peak before Australia's fast-bowling pair, Lillee and Thomson, rode roughshod over them; and finally the enigmatic West Indies team were moulded by captain Clive Lloyd into a champion combination of batting, bowling and fielding that dominated the game for years to come.

In 1977, the cricket world was turned upside down by Kerry Packer. The Australian media mogul had heard the frustrations of the leading players of the time—headed by Ian Chappell's Australian team —who wanted a 'better deal'. Packer had the means (wealth) and know-how (business) and grabbed the game by the scruff of the neck and gave it an almighty shake. Cricket would never be the same … but it would be a much stronger game.

Retro Cricket is a celebration of the game from the end of World War II to the end of the 1970s … the great series, the very best players, the controversies and the amazing crowd-filled ovals. With many new and rarely seen images it is a book for all generations to be enjoyed by those who love the game, no matter what age. Take a stroll through cricket's sporting history; enjoy the retro years of cricket before the game was changed forever and became the multi-million dollar, year-round sporting roller-coaster it is today.

Ian Collis, October 2014

Above: Under fading light, comes one of the more unusual cricket photos you would see. It is 1944 and with war still raging in Europe a bomb falls in the vicinity, during the Army v RAF match played at Lord's. The players can be seen ducking against the blast. Just after this, in true British spirit the players got to their feet and play quickly resumed.

SEASON	OPPONENTS	RESULT	No. TESTS
1945/46	AUSTRALIA in NEW ZEALAND	AUSTRALIA 1-0	1
1946	INDIA in ENGLAND	ENGLAND 1-0	3
1946/47	THE ASHES (ENGLAND in AUSTRALIA)	AUSTRALIA 3-0	5
	ENGLAND in NEW ZEALAND	DRAWN 0-0	1
1947	SOUTH AFRICA in ENGLAND	ENGLAND 3-0	5
1947/48	INDIA in AUSTRALIA	AUSTRALIA 4-0	5
	ENGLAND in WEST INDIES	WEST INDIES 2-0	4
1948	THE ASHES (AUSTRALIA in ENGLAND)	AUSTRALIA 4-0	5
1948/49	WEST INDIES in INDIA	WEST INDIES 1-0	5
	ENGLAND in SOUTH AFRICA	ENGLAND 2-0	5
1949	NEW ZEALAND in ENGLAND	DRAWN 0-0	4
1949/50	AUSTRALIA in SOUTH AFRICA	AUSTRALIA 4-0	5

Right: Len Hutton (left) and Cyril Washbrook go out to open the batting for England in the 1940s at Old Trafford.

Below: The great Indian batsman of the day, Vijay Merchant walking out to bat.

Below: The South Africa team taking the field on 9 June 1947 at Trent Bridge against England on the second day after being all out for 533 in their first innings.

Right: Crowds anxiously waiting in the rain at the SCG for a decision as to whether there would be any play on the second day of the fifth Test between Australia and India in March 1947.

Left: Norman Yardley, the England captain, dances with excitement as Hutton makes a great effort to take a chance offered by Viljoen during South Africa's second innings in the final Test match at The Oval in August 1947. The bowler is Dick Howarth with Mitchell (South Africa) at the other end.

Below: The 1948 Australian Test team...The Invincibles. Back Row (L to R): R. Lindwall, K. Miller, W. Brown. Middle Row: W. Ferguson (scorer and baggage man), N. Harvey, D. Ring, E. Toshack, W. Johnson, R. Saggers, G. Johnson (manager). Front Row: S. Loxton, R. Hammence, L. Hassett, D. Bradman (captain), C. McCool, A. Morris, I. Johnson. D. Tallon does not appear in this photograph.

Above: The great Don Bradman bids farewell to England at the end of the 1948 tour to England in September.

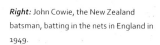

Right: John Cowie, the New Zealand batsman, batting in the nets in England in 1949.

Right: Returning from active duty during the war, Keith Miller, the tear-away bowler and damaging batsmen would be part of a bold new era of Australian post-war cricket.

1950S CRICKET TESTS:

SEASON	OPPONENTS	RESULT	No. TESTS
1950	WEST INDIES in ENGLAND	WEST INDIES 3-1	4
1950/51	THE ASHES (ENGLAND in AUSTRALIA)	AUSTRALIA 4-1	5
	ENGLAND in NEW ZEALAND	ENGLAND 1-0	2
1951	SOUTH AFRICA in ENGLAND	ENGLAND 3-1	5
1951/52	WEST INDIES in AUSTRALIA	AUSTRALIA 4-1	5
	ENGLAND in INDIA	DRAWN 1-1	5
	WEST INDIES in NEW ZEALAND	WEST INDIES 1-0	2
1952	INDIA in ENGLAND	ENGLAND 3-0	4
1952/53	PAKISTAN in INDIA	INDIA 2-1	5
	SOUTH AFRICA in AUSTRALIA	DRAWN 2-2	5
	SOUTH AFRICA in NEW ZEALAND	SOUTH AFRICA 1-0	2
	INDIA in WEST INDIES	WEST INDIES 1-0	5
1953	THE ASHES (AUSTRALIA in ENGLAND)	ENGLAND 1-0	5
1953/54	NEW ZEALAND in SOUTH AFRICA	SOUTH AFRICA 4-0	5
	ENGLAND in WEST INDIES	DRAWN 2-2	5
1954	PAKISTAN in ENGLAND	DRAWN 1-1	4
1954/55	INDIA in PAKISTAN	DRAWN 0-0	5
	THE ASHES (ENGLAND in AUSTRALIA)	ENGLAND 3-1	5
	ENGLAND in NEW ZEALAND	ENGLAND 2-0	2
1955	AUSTRALIA in WEST INDIES	AUSTRALIA 3-0	5
	SOUTH AFRICA in ENGLAND	ENGLAND 3-2	5
1955/56	NEW ZEALAND in PAKISTAN	PAKISTAN 2-0	3
	NEW ZEALAND in INDIA	INDIA 2-0	5
	WEST INDIES in NEW ZEALAND	WEST INDIES 3-1	4
1956	THE ASHES (AUSTRALIA in ENGLAND)	ENGLAND 2-1	5
1956/57	AUSTRALIA in PAKISTAN	PAKISTAN 1-0	1
	AUSTRALIA in INDIA	AUSTRALIA 2-0	3
	ENGLAND in SOUTH AFRICA	DRAWN 2-2	5
1957	WEST INDIES in ENGLAND	ENGLAND 3-0	5
1957/58	AUSTRALIA in SOUTH AFRICA	AUSTRALIA 3-0	5
	PAKISTAN in WEST INDIES	WEST INDIES 3-1	5
1958	NEW ZEALAND in ENGLAND	ENGLAND 4-0	5
1958/59	WEST INDIES in INDIA	WEST INDIES 3-0	5
	THE ASHES (ENGLAND in AUSTRALIA)	AUSTRALIA 4-0	5
	ENGLAND in NEW ZEALAND	ENGLAND 1-0	2
	WEST INDIES in PAKISTAN	PAKISTAN 2-1	3
1959	INDIA in ENGLAND	ENGLAND 5-0	5
1959/60	AUSTRALIA in PAKISTAN	AUSTRALIA 2-0	3
	AUSTRALIA in INDIA	AUSTRALIA 2-1	5

Above: Ian Johnson (second from left) and Lindsay Hassett (on his left) are guests at a South Melbourne cricket club function in 1950.

Previous spread: At the third Test between England and the West Indies, Gilbert Parkhouse plays a ball from Frank Worrell, while John Dewes is the other batsman.

Right: Action from the first Test between England and the West Indies at Old Trafford in June 1950. Trevor Bailey after making 82 not out for England, smartly fields a ball from Stollmeyer off Hollies when the West Indies opened their innings.

Below: England's Alec Bedser clean bowls Clyde Walcott for just 8 on the third day of the third Test in July 1950.

Right: There were some real doubts about the state of the wicket in the first Test at Old Trafford, when England defeated the West Indies by 202 runs in 1950. The general dryness of the pitch is evident as T.G. Evans and H. Doggart chase a ball from Walcott.

Above: The MCC on board *Stratheden* steaming towards Australia for the 1950–51 Ashes series. On board ship Denis Compton (suitably attired), and recovering from a knee injury, was a regular on the sports deck, playing golf, with Godfrey Evans the England wicket-keeper waiting his turn.

Left: There was an early setback for England in the third Test against the West Indies in 1950 as Reg Simpson was caught Walcott off Johnson for 4 at Trent Bridge, much to the excitement of the fielding side.

Above: On 14 September 1950 the English tourists departed for Australia. Skipper F R Brown, recorded a message, with members of the MCC team on the sports deck of SS *Stratheden* at Tilbury before their departure. Reading from Compton (second from left) are Simpson, Bailey, Dewes, Sheppard, Warr, Hutton, Brown, Close, Bedser, McIntyre and Evans.

Above: Sir Donald Bradman and Lindsay Hassett confer at practice on the eve of the first Test.

Right: Captains Lindsay Hassett (left) and Freddie Brown toss the coin at Brisbane for the first Test in 1950. Hassett would win the toss and go on and also guide his side to a 70 run win. A tough series for captain Brown, who had been third choice after F.G. Mann and Norman Yardley had both been approached to captain the side, but had declined for business reasons. To add to this, his team was up against a formidable Australian side who were strong in batting and still had Lindwall, Miller and Johnson, the destroyers in 1948 under Bradman.

Above: Lindsay Hassett mobbed by fans when he came off to speak following the "We want Hassett" chant by thousands of fans at Melbourne in February 1951. Even though Australia lost this Test by 8 wickets to England, the series had been won 4–1.

Left: Clive Berrange Van Ryneveld, leg break bowler and all-rounder of the South African side played 19 Tests from 1951 to 1958. He took 17 Test wickets at 39.47 and scored 724 runs at 26.81.

Above: Australians Keith Miller and Don Tallon perform a juggling act after Freddie Brown had snicked a chance in the third Test at Sydney in January 1951. Tallon fumbled the ball, which Miller knocked back, but it hit Tallon on the chin and the chance was lost. Brown would go on to reach 79, before being bowled by Ray Lindwall, which would prove to be his highest score of the series.

Left: Clyde Walcott, the Barbados wicket-keeper and batsman and one of West Indies cricket's famous three 'Ws', of Walcott, Everton Weekes and Frank Worrell. Their averages in Tests were: Walcott 56.68 (44 Tests, 3798 runs); Weekes 58.61 (48 Tests, 4455 runs) and Worrell 49.98 (51 Tests, 3860 runs). No wonder they were famous!

Below: Godfrey Evans, the English and Kent wicket-keeper. He was rated by Wisden as 'arguably the best wicket-keeper the game has ever seen. He had 219 dismissals in 91 Tests between 1946 (debuting against India) and 1959 (also against India), becoming the first wicket-keeper to reach 200 dismissals and the first Englishman to reach both 1000 runs and 100 dismissals and subsequently 2000 runs and 200 dismissals in Test cricket.

Right: Dudley Nourse, the South African captain, pulling a ball from McMahon against Surrey in early June 1951. Nourse, also captained South Africa when the Australians visited after World War II. Lindsay Hassett's side proved far too good winning the series 4–0. Nourse however did all he could to keep his team competitive, heading his sides batting in the series with 405 runs at an average of 45, with a high score of 114 in the second Test at Cape Town.

Below: Dudley Nourse.

Left: Skipper of the South Africans, Dudley Nourse, pulls a ball from Surrey's John McMahon to leg during his score of 45 on the final days play of the tour match in June 1951. A few days later in the first Test Nourse would score a brilliant 208, belting 25 fours.

Right: First Test South Africa v England at Nottingham in June 1951. England opening pair Len Hutton (left) and Jack Ikin go out to bat to open their first innings. Ikin would fall cheaply for 1 while Hutton would score 63. South Africa would pull off a surprise win by 71 runs after scoring 483 and then just 121 in their second innings, with Bedser doing most of the damage taking 6–37. England had also scored heavily in their first innings with 419, and needed just 186 to win the Test. They would fall well short, dismissed for 114 with Eric Rowan (5–68) and 'Tufty' Mann (4–24) bowling the tourists to victory.

Above: On the third day of the first Test between England and South Africa, John Waite, the South African wicket-keeper tries to stump Denis Compton off Geoff Chubb's bowling.

Right: South Africa in England, first Test at Trent Bridge in 1951. England batsman Denis Compton is caught Waite bowled McCarthy for 112 after 320 minutes at the crease.

Left: The first day of the third Test match between England and South Africa. Waite is caught Ikin for 1 off Bedser after 45 minutes at the crease to have the tourists at 2-12.

Below: South Africa captain Dudley Nourse (left) and vice-captain Eric Rowan holding the mascot, a springbok after winning the first Test by 71 runs.

Above: Frank Worrell played 51 Tests for the West Indies from 1947–48 to 1963, scoring 3860 runs at an average of 49.48, which included 9 centuries and 22 fifties. He also took 69 wickets bowling either left-arm medium pace or slow. An extremely popular player, Worrell first captained his country on the famous 1960–61 tour of Australia. The Frank Worrell Trophy is now contested between the two countries.

Left: South Africa in England, 7 July 1951. Test match day three, Willie Watson well fielded in the slips off Athol Rowan. Note the South African field placements.

Right: Sonny Ramadhin, the West Indies spin bowler was secretive about his bowling grip but he gripped a pen to add his name to the others on a souvenir bat at the MCG in 1951. With him is Victorian Test bowler Ian Johnson.

Right: 20 September 1951. South African cricketers leaving Waterloo Station en-route for home. In the carriage window at the station can be seen players (Left to Right) Eric Rowan, Athol Rowan and Dudley Nourse (captain) with the Springbok mascot.

Left: Everton Weekes caught Langley bowled Lindwall for a duck at the SCG in the fifth Test between the West Indies and Australia in the 1951–52 season. After dismissing Australia for 116 in their first innings the Windies were dismissed for just 78, before eventually losing the Test by 202 runs and the series 4–1.

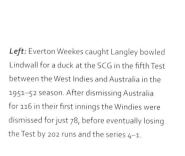

Left: Richie Benaud began his Test career on 25 January 1952 against the West Indies in the fifth Test in Sydney. His scored 3 and 19 in the two innings and took 1–14 in the Windies second innings. Needless to say his Test career would dramatically improve in the years to come finishing with 248 wickets at 27.03 with a career best in an innings of 7–72, plus he scored 2201 runs, which included 3 centuries and 9 fifties with a high score of 122.

Right: Len Hutton receives a tray of telegrams upon his appointment as the first professional England captain in 1952.

Above: Alfred Louis Valentine who played 36 Test for the West Indies from 1950 to 1957, wearing his WI cap and jersey. The left-arm spinner was the leading wicket-taker for both sides in the 1951–52 series with 24, with best figures of 6–102 in the third Test at Adelaide.

Right: Alf Valentine of the West Indies, in Australia at SCG No 2 nets.

Above: The South African team which toured Australia during the Australian summer of 1952–53 and who would draw the series 2–2 with wins in the second and fifth Tests, both at Melbourne. The squad in no particular order was: J.E. Cheetham (captain), D.J. McGlew (vice-captain), W.R. Endean, E.R.H. Fuller, K.J. Funston, G. Innes, H.J. Keith, P.N.F. Mansell, R.A. McLean, M.G. Melle, A.R.A. Murray, E.B. Norton, H.J. Tayfield, J.H.B. Waite, J.C. Watkins, K. Viljoen (manager).

Above: An Australian XI who played against the touring South Africans in December 1952. Standing (left to right): S.J. Carroll, A.K. Davidson, G.B. Hole, R.G. Archer, R. Benaud. Seated: I.D. Craig, unidentified, I.H. McDonald, P.L. Ridings, J.W. Burke, unidentified, C.C. McDonald. In a drawn match the Australian XI scored 372 (Hole 97, C. McDonald 81) and 200 for 4 (Carroll 79) and South Africa 296 (McGlew 74, Cheetham 52).

Above: The 1953 Australian team line up in England before a match. From left to right: A. L. Hassett (captain), A.R. Morris, G.B. Hole, J De Courcy, W.A. Johnston, J.C. Hill, A.K. Davidson, G.R. Langley, R. Benaud, I.D. Craig, R.N. Harvey.

Above: Lindsay Hassett practices on the grass outside while Hugh Tayfield and Hedley Keith bat in the nets a day before the start of the second Test in Melbourne of the 1952–53 Test series.

Right: After debuting for Australia in the fifth Test against South Africa, Ron Archer, the Queensland all-rounder was selected for the 1953 tour of England.

Above: Australia v South Africa; Arthur Morris, Ian Craig, Ron Archer of Australia with Hedley Keith of South Africa during the fifth Test of the series at the Australians hotel. Although Australia scored 520 on their first innings, with Neil Harvey top-scoring with 205, South Africa would come away with a 6 wicket win to square the five Test series 2–2.

Above: The 1953 Australian touring team to England. In no particular order: A.L. Hassett (captain), A.R. Morris (vice-captain), R.G. Archer. R. Benaud, I.D. Craig, A.K. Davidson, J.H. De Courcy, R.N. Harvey, J.C. Hill, G.B. Hole, W.A. Johnston, G.R. Langley, R.R. Lindwall, K.R. Miller, C.C. McDonald, D.T. Ring, D. Tallon, G.A. Davies (manager).

Above: The Australian cricket team pictured on board *Orcades* on their arrival at Southampton in April. The captain, Lindsay Hassett and manager G.A. Davies are in the front centre.

Right: Ship's commander Captain
N.A. Whinfield and Australia cricket team
captain Lindsay Hassett at Southampton.
Whinfield's ship, the Orient liner *Orcades*
has just arrived with the cricketers, in the
background (centre with hat is Doug Ring,
Victorian bowler and batsman). Behind
Hassett is Keith Miller, while on the right
is Ian Craig in the dark raincoat.

Below: The 1953 Australian cricketers
at Southampton. Hassett (left) is with
17-year-old Ian Craig, the youngest player to
represent Australia in a Test match.

Left: The Duke of Edinburgh seems to be thoroughly enjoying a joke with the Australian cricketers, Keith Miller and Lindsay Hassett at East Molesey Memorial Ground on April 26. The Australians opened their tour with a charity one-day match against the East Molesey team and the Duke was introduced to the players during the tea interval.

Left: Australian and English cricketers on the links at Burnham, Buckinghamshire in April 1953. (L to R): England's Jim Laker, Australia's Alan Davidson, former Australian Test cricketer Ben Barnett and Australia's Bill Johnston.

Right: The Australians take the field to open the English tour at East Molesey, Surrey. The players are (left to right): A.L. Hassett (captain), J. De Courcy, A.R. Morris, R. Benaud, R.N. Harvey, D.T. Ring, W.A. Johnston, R.R. Lindwall and almost hidden D. Tallon.

Left: Ron Archer and other Australians appeal to the umpire for a catch behind the wicket against Constable during the Surrey tour match, which was upheld. In the action can be seen, from left to right: Ring, Davidson, Benaud, Hole, De Courcey and Tallon. Australia would win the match by an innings and 76 runs with Archer starring with the ball, taking 6–26 and 5–35.

Above: Neil Harvey is caught by wicket-keeper John Asquith off the bowling of Thomas Hare for 25 runs in the Cambridge v Australian tour match in May. Australia won by an innings and 106 runs.

Left: Lindsay Hassett, the Australian Test captain had intensive practice at the Lord's nets two days before the upcoming first Test which was at Nottingham. It must have made a difference as he scored 115 in his sides first innings of just 249. The match finished in a draw.

Below: The first Test Australia in England on the opening morning at Trent Bridge, Nottingham. Opener Graeme Hole is bowled by Alec Bedser for 0, leaving Australia at 1 wicket down for 2 runs. Arthur Morris and Lindsay Hassett quickly rectified the situation, putting on 122 for the second wicket.

Left: The Australians appeal for lbw against England's Trevor Bailey in the first Test of the 1953 Ashes series. At top is Australia's wicket-keeper Don Tallon. Surrey bowler Alec Bedser took seven Australian wickets for 44 runs in the third days play, which brought his figures for the two innings to 14 wickets for just 99 runs. He set up an English Test wicket-taking record, reaching 196, surpassing the previous best of 189 by Sidney Barnes. At the end of play England needed just 187 runs with nine second innings wickets in hand. Unfortunately for the home side, a washed-out fourth day and a delayed start on the fifth meant England could only play out time.

Left: Ray Lindwall slashes one round to leg in the second Test of 1953 against England. The progress of the ball is watched by keeper Godfrey Evans and England captain Len Hutton. Australia ended the fourth day at Lord's with their tails well up, 322 runs ahead and three of England's best wickets down for only 20. Ray Lindwall got Len Hutton and Don Kenyon caught for a personal cost of just seven runs. This was after he had scored 50 runs in his sides second innings. Bill Johnston bowling at the other end got Tom Graveney caught in the slips. England however, held out on the final day, finishing at 7-282, with Watson top-scoring with 109.

Above: A fresh faced 23 year-old Alan Davidson touring England in May 1953. A fast-medium left hand bowler and very useful bat who would go on and have a brilliant Test career, eventually taking 186 wickets and scoring 1328 runs.

Left: Lindsay Hassett is dropped during his innings of 104 by Denis Compton in the first innings of the second Test at Lord's. Godfrey Evans is the wicketkeeper who rues the missed chance.

Above: Neil Harvey is caught Godfrey Evans off Alec Bedser for 122 at Old Trafford, Manchester in the third Test of the series, with again the match ending in a draw.

Left: England's W.J. Edrich is given a rousing ovation after making a fighting 64 before being caught Jim De Courcy, blowed Lindwall, on the fourth day of the fourth Test at Leeds against Australia. For the fourth Test in a row, there was still no result, heading into the final Test.

Above: Australia's Keith Miller makes a great catch off Bill Johnston to dismiss Surrey's Stewart Surridge for a duck at Kennigton Oval, London. Don Tallon the wicket-keeper keeps a close eye on Miller's effort.

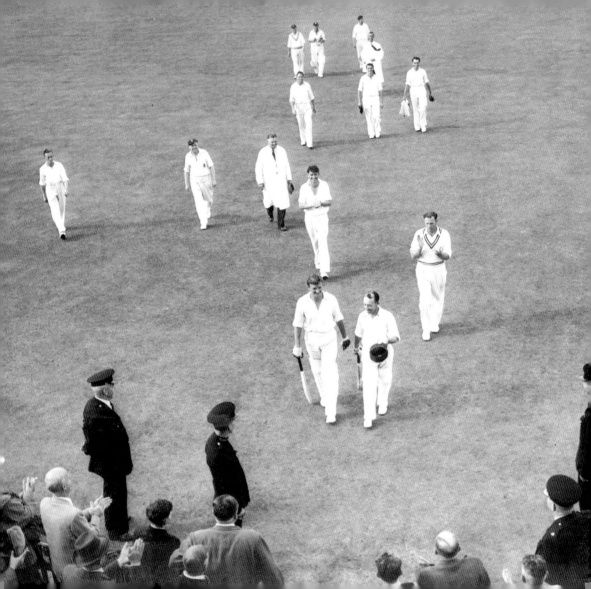

Right: Rival captains Lindsay Hassett and Len Hutton toss the coin at Kennington Oval for the fifth and final Test.

Left: Australian's unbeaten batsmen Lindsay Hassett and Richie Benaud and the Warwickshire team coming in at the conclusion of the match.

Above: Keith Miller is caught by England's Freddie Trueman bowled Laker in the second innings at The Oval in the fifth Test for a duck as England take command.

Right: Her Majesty the Queen shaking hands with G. Hole of the Australian team, introduced by Lindsay Hassett. On the left is G. Davies, the team manager.

Above: August 1953. Ray Lindwall bowling at The Oval during the final and most vital Test between England and Australia. He would go on and take the wickets of Edrich, Compton, Graveney and Lock in the first innings.

Right: Hutton batting to an Australian field of Morris, De Courcey, Archer, Hole, Miller, Langley and Hassett, and has also lost his cap in the process. A solid captain's knock by Hutton would prove decisive in England winning the fifth Test and the series 1–0.

Previous spread: The Australian fielders wait in an arch round the wicket as Hutton plays a ball from Miller through the slips at the start of the second days play at The Oval. Hutton would go on to top score with 82 to guide his side to a narrow 31 run first innings lead, Lock and Laker would scuttle the Australians in their second innings to run out convincing winners.

Below: Bill Edrich is out lbw for 21 to Ray Lindwall during the morning of the second days play to have England at 1-37 in reply to Australia's first innings score of 275, with the match evenly balanced.

Above: Freddie Trueman hits a boundary off
Johnston during the final Test at The Oval on
the third day.

Left: The dust rises as Keith Miller bowls to Trevor Bailey on the third day of the vital last Test match of the series.

Left: Bill Edrich hits a ball from Johnston for four runs. Wicket-keeper Langley follows the path of the ball during the final Test at The Oval on the fourth day. Ray Lindwall is at point and Alan Davidson is at short leg.

Right: Victorious not out batsmen Denis Compton and Bill Edrich leave the pitch after England win the Ashes at The Oval.

Left: Denis Compton and Bill Edrich leave the pitch through a cordon of bobbies as the huge crowd makes way after England win the Ashes, August 1953.

Following spread: In a sea of euphoria the huge crowd celebrate on the pitch at The Oval after England win the Ashes.

Left: The crowd at The Oval in 1953 after England regained The Ashes.

Above: On 24 September Lindsay Hassett backed by his team, makes a farewell speech (notice cine-camera and TV also) on the deck of the Strathaird at Tilbury, when the team left for home.

Above: In a change of scenery for the English cricketers, Fred Trueman and Tom Graveney relaxing in the West Indies.

Above: A rare shot as Len Hutton bats on matted wicket in the West Indies.

Right: The MCC touring team in the West Indies 1953–54.

Below: Jeff Stollmeyer (left) and Michael Frederick (on Test debut) walk out to open the innings for the West Indies against England in the first Test at Sabina Park, Jamaica, 23 January 1954. While Frederick would fall to Statham for a duck, Stollmeyer scored an invaluable 60 before also falling to Statham.

Right: Watson sweeps round at a ball from Gomez during his 116 for England in the second innings. It was all to no avail as England lost the opening Test match of the series by 140 runs.

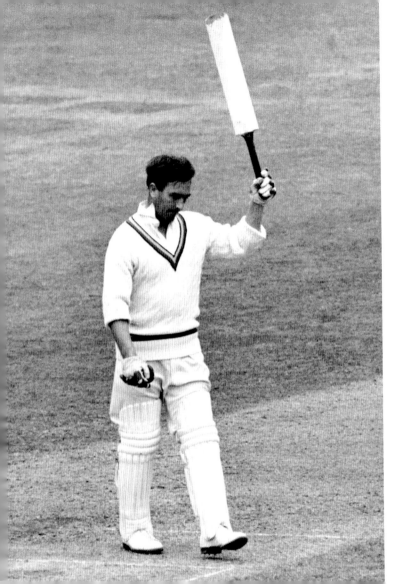

Left: After the First Test was drawn due to some inclement weather in the England and Pakistan Test series starting in June, England gained the ascendancy by winning the second test by an innings and 129 runs. Dismissing Pakistan for 157, England responded with 558 runs, led brilliantly by Denis Compton as he raises his bat having reached his century. He would go on to score his highest Test innings of 278, with 34 fours and 1 six. Pakistan would eventually surprise the home side by winning the fourth Test by a mere 24 runs to tie the series at 1–1.

Right: The England team on their boat after arriving in Australia for the 1954–55 Ashes series.

Left: The 1954–55 MCC Team to Australia. In no particular order the squad was: L. Hutton (captain), P.B.H. May (vice-captain), K.V. Andrew, R. Appleyard, T.E. Bailey, A.V. Bedser, D.C.S. Compton, M.C. Cowdrey, W.J. Edrich, T.G. Evans, T.W. Graveney, P.J. Loder, J.E. McConnon, R.T. Simpson, J.B. Statham, F.H. Tyson, J.H. Wardle, J.V. Wilson.

Below: In October, a little golf was the order of the day as Tyson (Northants), Statham (Lancashire) and Wardle and Appleyard (Yorkshire) seen at Royal Perth Golf Club after the team arrived at Fremantle.

Right: Neil Harvey is caught Godfrey Evans bowled Statham for 4 in the match between Australia XI and MCC in November 1954 in Melbourne. With two of the four days washed out the match ended in a draw with England 205 in their only innings and Australia XI, 7-167 in reply.

Below: Bill Edrich gets in some batting practice at the WACA in Perth in November.

Left: New South Wales batsman Richie Benaud survives an lbw appeal from England's Brian Statham at Sydney in a tour match on England's 1954–55 tour. Looking at the photo you would have to ask how did he survive?

Below: Keith Miller receives ray treatment for his knee injury from masseur Charlie O'Brien as he tries to get fit for the second Test of the 1954–55 series against England in Sydney. Unfortunately for Miller he didn't play and Australia lost the match by 38 runs.

Above: Australia's famous Melbourne Cricket
Ground is always a special place to be when
an Ashes Test match is being played.

Left: Australia v England, in the third Test at Melbourne in January 1955. Les Favell is out lbw to Brian Statham for 25 during Australia's first innings of 231 in reply to England's 191. A second innings collapse by Australia courtesy of a Frank Tyson onslaught, taking 7–27 saw England takes a 2–1 series lead with two to play.

Right: Bill Edrich is been bowled by Bill Johnston for 13 during England's second innings. They would go on to score 279, setting Australia 240 to win.

Following spread: April 1955. In brilliant sunshine, members of the champion Surrey team walk to the nets at The Oval to get some practice in preparation for another season. Left to right: Ken Barrington, Eric Bedser, David Fletcher, Michael Stewart, Arthur McIntyre, Stuart Surridge, Peter Loader and Bernie Constable.

Right: Ian Johnson (Australian captain) and England's vice-captain Peter May sign autograph books while they waited for a decision whether play would take place in the fifth Test at the SCG in February 1955. A rain-drenched Sydney saw no start to play until 2pm on day four.

Left: Australian Selectors Dudley Seddon (left), Sir Donald Bradman and Jack Ryder watch the fourth Test between Australia and England at Adelaide Oval in February 1955. They were to announce the Australian team for the fifth Test the following day. This was a Test series England won 3–1.

Right: Colin Cowdrey batting with a broken nose, faces Keith Miller's bowling on the fifth day of the fourth Test in 1955. Although he would fall to Miller a few deliveries later for just 4, his 79 in the first innings helped pave the way for an England victory and an unassailable 3–1 lead in the series with just the final Test remaining.

Below: In his mid-30s but still regarded as one of the world's best all-rounders, Keith Miller cuts English fast bowler Brian Statham through the gully past Colin Cowdrey in the fourth Test of the 1954–55 Test series.

Below: Captain's Len Hutton (left) and Ian Johnson were thwarted by the Sydney weather in the fifth Test of the 1954–55 series. The series did not prove to be a good one for the home side, losing 3–1 to England, with the pace duo of 'Typhoon' Frank Tyson and Brian Statham far too good for Australia's batsmen.

Right: The packed SCG in Sydney during the Ashes Tests in 1954–55. There were two Tests played there, the second Test in December, which England won by 38 runs, and the fifth Test in February, which was drawn.

Left: After Australia won the first Test by 9 wickets at Kingston, in March, Everton Weekes (pictured) and Clyde Walcott scored centuries in the first innings at Port-Of-Spain, Trinidad to ensure an honourable draw against the big-hitting Australians, who responded with a first innings of 600. Weekes can be seen hitting a four during his hard-hitting 139, on the second day during the Test.

Left: Arthur Morris, a left-handed opening bat, who played Test cricket for Australia from 1946 until 1955. He was only 18 when he scored a century in each innings of his first-class debut for NSW in 1940. He debuted for Australia in the 1946–47 Test series against England and made a brilliant start, reeling off three centuries in a row – the second innings of the third Test (155), then in each innings in the fourth Test (122 and 124 not out). In all Morris would go on to play 46 Tests, scoring 3533 runs at an average of 46.48, with his highest score of 206 coming against England in the fourth Test at Adelaide in the 1950–51 series.

Left: Allan Rae (Jamaica) and Ian Johnson (Australia) toss in their tour match in June 1955. Rae, who had played Test cricket for the West Indies from 1948 to 1953, was a top-order left-hand batsman.

Above: Ian Johnson and Frank Worrell are among those to inspect the wicket before play during the Australians 1954–55 tour to the West Indies.

Left: Clyde Walcott gives a wry grimace as he is bowled by Richie Benaud for 83 during the final day of the fourth Test against Australia at Bridgetown, Barbados in 1955. In the background is Bill Watson (fielding), and Gil Langley (wicket-keeper). Match scores were: Australia 668 and 249; West Indies 510 and 6-234. Match drawn.

Above: West Indian captain Jeff Stollmeyer slashes one through the slips which Neil Harvey fails to stop. Everton Weekes also joined in with a boundary laden innings as soon as he came in just half an hour before stumps on the first day of the second Test match against Australia at picturesque Queen's Park Ground. Nearly 30,000 spectators cheered Weekes as he hit to boundary six times in his score of 27 runs.

Left: The third Test in July 1955, between South Africa and England at Old Trafford. Don Kenyon is caught at the wicket by Waite off Heine for 5 in England's first innings total of 284. Left to right are Tayfield, Goddard, Mansell and Waite. South Africa would win the Test by 3 wickets.

Below: Frank Tyson playing for England v South Africa. In terms of raw pace, there have been few bowlers in the game's history to match England's Frank Tyson. Against South Africa in just two Tests Tyson captured 14 wickets, with best figures of 6–28 at Nottingham in the first Test. In a career spanning 17 Tests from 1954–59 he captured 76 wickets at a wicked average of just 18.56 .

Above: England captain Peter May just fails to get his fingers to a chance from Goddard as he gets a Lock delivery away at the start of the South African innings at The Oval. Goddard's luck would not last long though as he was soon dismissed for 8, lbw to Bailey and the South Africans would be dismissed for just 112. After England had won the opening two Tests, South Africa levelled the series with wins in both the third and fourth Tests. England took the series at The Oval with a 92 run win, with bowlers Laker and Lock doing the damage.

Right: The opening morning of the fifth Test at The Oval. The South African team are led out by Jack Cheetham for the start of the deciding Test match against England with the rubber standing at 2–2.

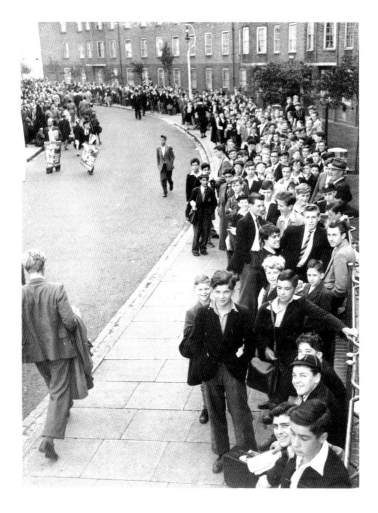

Left: After the rain on Saturday, the crowd was determined to make the most of what looked like a sunny day, and here was the scene from the vicinity of The Oval well before the start of play, with spectators keen to watch the decider in this exciting series.

Right: With the rain now gone, the huge crowd sits in the fine English sunshine watching the deciding Test of the 1955 series.

Above: Ian Johnson (Australian captain) and the Rev David Sheppard, former England and Sussex cricketer, tossing the coin before the start of the match between the Australians and The Duke of Norfolk's XI at Arundel Castle in 1956. Ian and his team had arrived in the country four days earlier and had since been busy attending receptions and the like.

Left: Heine appeals to umpire Dai Davies, and Lock is given out lbw for 1 in England's second innings of 204, setting South Africa 244 to win the test and take the series. South Africa would fall 92 runs short managing just 151.

Above: Up goes the coin toss, which would be won by Sheppard, who decided to bat in the first game of the tour of England in the grounds of Arundel Castle, Sussex. Australia won the match 7-189 to 188.

Right: In their second match of the tour on 4 May against Worcestershire, Ray Lindwall hits a four. In a match Worcestershire just hung on for a draw, Benaud top-scored for the tourists with 160 in his sides total of 9-438 declared against the locals 90 and 9-231.

Above: The Australian team just before leaving Melbourne for Tasmania and then on to England. They are (left to right): Arthur James (masseur), W. J. Dowling (manager), Len Maddocks, Alan Davidson, Ian Craig, Ken Mackay, John Rutherford, Jim Burke, Neil Harvey, Keith Miller,

Ian Johnson (captain), Peter Burge, Ray Lindwall, Pat Crawford, Colin MacDonald, Richie Benaud, Ron Archer, J Wilson, W.L. Rush (assistant manager), Gil Langley and N. Gorman (scorer and baggage man).

Previous spread: The entire Australian side can be seen in the field against Cambridge at Fenners, Cambridge on a May morning in 1956. Fast bowler Archer is square cut by Wilenkin, at one of the world's most beautiful cricket grounds.

Left: MCC v Australia at Lord's in late May. Congratulations from MCC captain R.T. Simpson (left) and vanquished MCC bowler Alan Moss to Neil Harvey and Jack Rutherford as they come in for tea after putting on 218 for the second wicket.

Right: Ian Johnson is delighted as Surrey batsman Ken Barrington is caught by Keith Miller during the tour match in May 1956. Barrington had batted tediously for over an hour for just four runs. But he had the last laugh with Surrey winning the three-day match by 10 wickets. Interestingly, in Australia's first innings of 259, Surrey off-spinner Jim Laker gave an indication of what was to come in the Test series, claiming all 10 wickets for 88 runs off 46 overs.

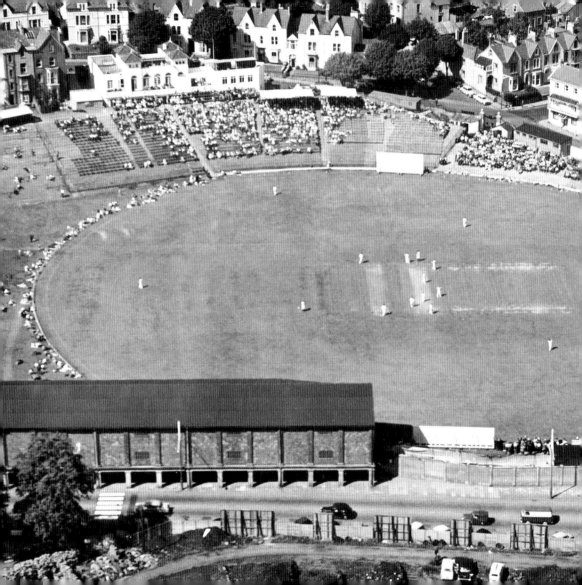

Above: A wonderful aerial view of the St Helen's cricket ground in Swansea, Wales during the 1956 season.

Below: A very scarce image of Denis Compton bowling left handed during the 1956 English season.

Left: On day three of the second Test at Lord's, England captain Peter May cuts a ball from Keith Miller past Richie Benaud for a single. He would top score for his side with 63 in the first innings before being bowled by Benaud.

Below: Australian wicket-keeper Gil Langley padding up in England.

Above: Peter Burge clean bowled by Statham for 21 on the second day of the second Test at Lord's. Australia won the Test by 185 runs to take a 1–0 lead in the series after the first Test at Nottingham was drawn. Keith Miller proved the hero for Australia with a 10 wicket haul (5-72 in the first innings and 5-80 in the second).

Below: Lillian an eight month old kangaroo is the centre of attraction to members of the Australian Test touring team, who were guests of honour at a cocktail party at Kensington Palace Hotel, London, given by a cricket fan, Kenneth Wood, 39 year-old director of a manufacturing company. At Left is Ian Johnson (Australian captain). Second right is Beverley Prowse, 22, Australian beauty queen (Miss Victoria 1956), who was also a guest at the party. The host of the party, Kenneth Wood, is a keen Surrey supporter, the country team the Australian side was playing at the time.

Right: Australia in England, at Lord's June 1956. An unusual view of the Lord's ground during the Test match, taken from the top of the apartments overlooking the Mount Stand.

Above: England XI v Australia at Lord's, 1956. Back Row (L to R): F.S. Trueman, J.H. Wardle, T.W. Graveney, J.B. Statham, M.C. Cowdrey, P.E. Richardson. Front Row: W. Watson, T.E. Bailey, P.B.H. May (captain), J.C. Laker, T.G. Evans.

Above: The 1956 Australian touring side at Lord's. In no particular order: I.W. Johnson (captain), K.R. Miller (vice-captain), R.G. Archer, R. Benaud, P.J. Burge, J.W. Burke, I.D. Craig, P. Crawford, A.K. Davidson, R.N. Harvey, G.R. Langley, R.R. Lindwall, K. Mackay, L.V. Maddocks, C.C. McDonald, J. Rutherford, J. Wilson.

Below: England spinner Tony Lock appeals for a wicket, with Australian batsman Keith Miller at the bowler's end during the 1956 Ashes tour.

Right: In the second Test Peter May is caught behind by Langley off Miller for 53 in the second innings.

Below: Ian Johnson and Keith Miller proudly display their MBEs after they had attended an investiture ceremony at Buckingham Palace in July 1956.

Right: England captain Peter May presents HRH Queen Elizabeth to Fred Trueman at Lord's in the 1956 England v Australia Test match.

Left: The 1956 Australian's walking onto the field at Old Trafford during the 1956 Ashes Tour, led by captain Ian Johnson and Keith Miller to his left.

Below: Jim Laker is applauded off the oval after his 19 wickets in the fourth Test at Old Trafford. His full bowling figures for the match were: first innings, 16.4 overs, 4 maidens, 37 runs for 9 wickets; second innings, 51.2 overs, 23 maidens, 53 runs for 10 wickets. England won the Test by an innings and 170 runs to take a 2–1 lead in the series after winning the third Test at Leeds, where Laker and Lock destroyed the tourists.

Left: A typical field set by Australian captain Ian Johnson, as England opener Peter Richardson receives a ball from Ray Lindwall. Richardson would go on to score 37 in the first innings and 34 in the second in a low scoring match. With a draw here in the fifth Test England won the series 2–1.

Below: Keith Miller winces after being struck on the body from a ball by Brian Statham (who stands emotionless) on the second day of the fifth Test at The Oval. Miller would go on and top score for Australia in the first innings with a well compiled 61 to help deny the home side a victory.

Above: Keith Miller (right) lashes out at a
ball from Brian Statham in the fifth Test.
England fielders are (L to R) David Sheppard,
Peter May, Colin Cowdrey and wicket-keeper
Godfrey Evans.

Below: Alan Davidson catches Frank Tyson off the bowling of Ron Archer in the fifth Test at The Oval. The wicket-keeper is Gil Langley, with Keith Miller standing to his right.

Below: A tense moment as Australian captain Ian Johnson is given not out on a ball from Jim Laker at The Oval. In the action can be seen (left to right) the umpire, Jim Laker, Neil Harvey, English captain Peter May, unidentified fielder (back to camera), Tony Lock, wicket-keeper Godfrey Evans and Ian Johnson.

Right: Ian Craig was appointed as the youngest ever captain of Australia at 21 for the tour to South Africa. Seen here training as a pharmacist in England after the news of his selection in May 1957. While he would lead Australia to a 3–0 series win, his own form with the bat was disappointing, scoring just 103 runs at an average of 14.71 in the five Tests.

Right: Jim Laker traps Jim Burke lbw in Australia's second innings for 1. The 1956 Test series faded out before time with the weather victorious. The final match ended in a draw, with England desperately unlucky not to register another win. Final scores were: England 247 and 3-182 declared, Australia 202 and 5-27.

Above: Keith Miller would play his last Test for Australia later this year, in October against Pakistan in Karachi, and would remain one of the truly natural talents of Test cricket. In this image he has been bowled by England's Trevor Bailey in the second Test at Melbourne in the 1950–51 Ashes series. A Royal Australian Air Force pilot during World War II, Miller is widely regarded as Australia's greatest ever all-rounder. With great ability with both bat and ball, his general manner and good looks he was a great favourite. He played 55 Tests from 1946 to 1956, scored 2958 runs at 36.97, with a top score of 147, took 170 wickets at 22.97 with a personal best of 7–60. He was also a very good Australian rules footballer, playing 50 matches for St Kilda, but in summing him up, he loved the contest rather than the victory, and his larger than life rebellious nature helped both shape and possibly limit his cricket career.

Right: Clyde Walcott batting for West Indies against England in 1957. In 44 Tests he would score 3798 runs at an average of 56.68 with a high score of 220, with 15 hundreds and 14 fifties.

Above: West Indian Everton Weekes at Lord's in April. It was there in the second Test he would have his highest score of the series, a 90, hitting 16 fours. Nearing the end of his Test career (1948–1958) he played in 48 Tests, scoring 4455 runs at 58.61 with a high score of 207, with 15 hundreds and 19 fifties.

Left: The third Test between the West Indies and England at Trent Bridge. Garry Sobers swings and misses at a ball which also evades wicket-keeper Godfrey Evans. With England leading 1–0 in the series and scoring 619 in their first innings, the Windies did well to hang on for a draw and keep the series alive.

Right: England wrap up the series 3–0, with victories in the final two Tests. The Surrey pair, Tony Lock (5 for 28) and Jim Laker (3 for 29) are applauded off by players and crowd alike, dismissing the West Indies for 89 in the first innings of the Final Test in reply to England's 412. Between them is England and Surrey captain Peter May, while other players (L to R) are Loader, Bailey, Graveney, Sheppard, Cowdrey, Trueman, Evans and Richardson (extreme right).

Left: In the first Test between New Zealand and England at Edgbaston, the home side scored an emphatic 205 run victory. New Zealand batsman Playle is batting to a hostile field (L to R) of Cowdrey, Graveney, Evans, Smith, Lock, Laker, while Loader is in the foreground. The tourists would be dismissed for 94 and 137 in their two innings.

Below: New Zealand's N. Harford (left) and J. Reid coming out to bat against England in the Birmingham Test, 1958.

Above: Colin Cowdrey is caught by New Zealand skipper John Reid (next to wicket-keeper, Petrie) off a jubilant Hayes, after making 70 in the second innings, declaring at 6-215, setting the Kiwis 343.

Above: The MCC touring squad in Australia in 1958–59. In no particular order: P.B.H. May (captain), M.C. Cowdrey (vice-captain), T.E. Bailey, T.G. Evans, T.W. Graveney, J.C. Laker, P.J. Loader, G.A.R. Lock, C.A. Milton, P.E. Richardson, J.B. Statham, R. Subba Row, R. Swetman, F.S. Trueman, F.H. Tyson, W. Watson, J. Mortimore, E.R. Dexter, F. Brown (manager).

Above: The Australian team against England
for the Melbourne Test of the 1958–59 Ashes
series.

Below: The first morning of the fifth Test at The Oval, as New Zealand opener John D'Arcy gets Statham away. The other batsman is Lawrie Miller. With England already leading 4–0 in the series, rain would prevent a further loss here, with the home side again well on top.

Right: England v Combined XI at Perth. England captain Peter May cover drives McKay during his innings of 113.

Right: MCC opening pair Arthur Milton (left) and Peter Richardson walk out to open the innings against South Australia. They would have a century stand in the second innings and the tourists would win the match by 9 wickets.

Left: After Australia's emphatic victory on South African soil, captain Ian Craig contracted hepatitis and was unable to take his place in the series against England. In his place stepped Richie Benaud, who would have a great series 1958 back on home soil. Relying to England's first innings of just 134 in the first Test, Australian opener Jim Burke is out for 20, caught by Godfrey Evans off Peter Loader. Australia dominated with the ball, winning by 8 wickets.

Above: Australian bowler Ian Meckiff, who would capture 17 wickets at 17.82 (the best average by an Australian bowler in the series).

Right: NSW Bank employee Alan Davidson bowls England's Willie Watson for a duck in the first innings of the second Test. Davidson took three England wickets with the first, fifth and sixth balls of his second over for seven runs to have them reeling with just 7 runs on the board and 3 wickets down.

Above: England opener Peter Richardson looks around to see Australia's Neil Harvey take a great catch at second slip to dismiss him for 2 off the bowling of Ian Meckiff, during the fourth days play in the second Test in Melbourne. Australia again won the match by eight wickets to take a 2–0 lead in the series.

Above: Australian batsman Norman O'Neill square cuts a ball from Brian Statham for 3 during his innings of 77 in the first innings of the third Test. England would hang on here for a draw, their best result in the five Test series.

Left: Neil Marks (NSW) in his first international game, plays a defensive shot off Statham against the MCC at Sydney in January 1959. He would go on to make 46 before being bowled by Frank Tyson. The match was drawn with NSW 215 and 0-44 to MCC all out for 303.

Below: Captain Richie Benaud pulls Jim Laker for four to the mid-on boundary in the third Test at the SCG.

Below: Australian opener Colin McDonald is bowled by Trueman for a magnificent 170 in Australia's first innings total of 476 in the fourth Test, which would set-up a 10 wicket win and a 3–0 series lead.

Right: Alan Davidson drops his bat as he is hit on the leg by a ball from Trueman on the third day of the fourth Test. He would go on to score 43 invaluable runs.

Above: On the second morning of the fourth Test, Colin McDonald resumes his innings, after retiring injured at lunch on Saturday, and drives a ball from Statham. Burke is his runner, and he would go on and top score for Australia with 170.

Above: The end of England's second innings in the fourth Test as Godfrey Evans is caught by Richie Benaud off Alan Davidson for nought. England's total was 270, and it was all over bar the shouting with Australia needing just 35 runs to clinch the match and regain the Ashes they had lost in England in 1953. They got the runs without the loss of a wicket.

Right: Bowler Gordon Rorke and keeper Wally Grout, successfully shout a loud appeal for lbw against England captain Peter May, on the fifth day of the fourth Test. The appeal was upheld and May was out for 59.

Left: England fast bowler Frank Tyson, who bats at 9, is caught by Aussie keeper Wally Grout off skipper Richie Benaud, who throws his hands in the air in triumph. Despite Tyson's last-ditch stand of 33, England were all out for 270 and the Test was lost.

Below: Having retired from Test cricket for Australia, Keith Miller pulls a muscle while batting for the MCC against Oxford University, and is ceremonially carried from the field by members of the Oxford University team in June 1959.

Above: A great moment for Ray Lindwall,
snaring Trevor Bailey's wicket in the fifth
Test and breaking Clarrie Grimmett's record
for most wickets by an Australian in Tests.
Lindwall had dismissed Bailey without
scoring in both innings, this second time to
claim the record.

1960S CRICKET TESTS:

SEASON	OPPONENTS	RESULT	No. TESTS
1960	SOUTH AFRICA in ENGLAND	ENGLAND 3-0	5
1960/61	PAKISTAN in INDIA	DRAWN 0-0	5
	THE FRANK WORRELL TROPHY (WEST INDIES in AUSTRALIA)	AUSTRALIA 2-1	5
1961	THE ASHES (AUSTRALIA IN ENGLAND)	AUSTRALIA 2-1	5
1961/62	ENGLAND in INDIA	INDIA 2-0	5
	ENGLAND in PAKISTAN	ENGLAND 1-0	3
	NEW ZEALAND in SOUTH AFRICA	DRAWN 2-2	5
	INDIA in WEST INDIES	WEST INDIES 5-0	5
1962	PAKISTAN in ENGLAND	ENGLAND 4-0	5
1962/63	THE ASHES (ENGLAND IN AUSTRALIA)	DRAWN 1-1	5
	ENGLAND in NEW ZEALAND	ENGLAND 3-0	3

SEASON	OPPONENTS	RESULT	No. TESTS
1963	THE WISDEN TROPHY (WEST INDIES in ENGLAND)	WEST INDIES 3-1	5
1963/64	SOUTH AFRICA in AUSTRALIA	DRAWN 1-1	5
	ENGLAND in INDIA	DRAWN 0-0	5
	SOUTH AFRICA in NEW ZEALAND	DRAWN 0-0	3
1964	THE ASHES (AUSTRALIA in ENGLAND)	AUSTRALIA 1-0	5
1964/65	AUSTRALIA in INDIA	DRAWN 1-1	3
	AUSTRALIA in PAKISTAN	DRAWN 0-0	1
	PAKISTAN in AUSTRALIA	DRAWN 0-0	1
	PAKISTAN in NEW ZEALAND	DRAWN 0-0	3
	ENGLAND in SOUTH AFRICA	ENGLAND 1-0	5
	NEW ZEALAND in INDIA	INDIA 1-0	4
	NEW ZEALAND in PAKISTAN	PAKISTAN 2-0	3
	THE FRANK WORRELL TROPHY (AUSTRALIA in WEST INDIES)	WEST INDIES 2-1	5
1965	NEW ZEALAND in ENGLAND	ENGLAND 3-0	3
	SOUTH AFRICA in ENGLAND	SOUTH AFRICA 1-0	3
1965/66	THE ASHES (ENGLAND in AUSTRALIA)	DRAWN 1-1	5
	ENGLAND in NEW ZEALAND	DRAWN 0-0	3
1966	THE WISDEN TROPHY (WEST INDIES in ENGLAND)	WEST INDIES 3-1	5
1966/67	WEST INDIES in INDIA	WEST INDIES 2-0	3
	AUSTRALIA in SOUTH AFRICA	SOUTH AFRICA 3-1	5
1967	INDIA in ENGLAND	ENGLAND 3-0	3
	PAKISTAN in ENGLAND	ENGLAND 2-0	3
1967/68	INDIA in AUSTRALIA	AUSTRALIA 4-0	4
	INDIA in NEW ZEALAND	INDIA 3-1	4
	THE WISDEN TROPHY (ENGLAND in WEST INDIES)	ENGLAND 1-0	5
1968	THE ASHES (AUSTRALIA in ENGLAND)	DRAWN 1-1	5
1968/69	THE FRANK WORRELL TROPHY (WEST INDIES in AUSTRALIA)	AUSTRALIA 3-1	5
	ENGLAND in PAKISTAN	DRAWN 0-0	3
	WEST INDIES in NEW ZEALAND	DRAWN 1-1	3
1969	THE WISDEN TROPHY (WEST INDIES in ENGLAND)	ENGLAND 2-0	3
	NEW ZEALAND in ENGLAND	ENGLAND 2-0	3
1969/70	NEW ZEALAND in INDIA	DRAWN 1-1	3
	NEW ZEALAND in PAKISTAN	NEW ZEALAND 1-0	3
	AUSTRALIA in INDIA	AUSTRALIA 3-1	5
1969/70	AUSTRALIA in SOUTH AFRICA	SOUTH AFRICA 4-0	4

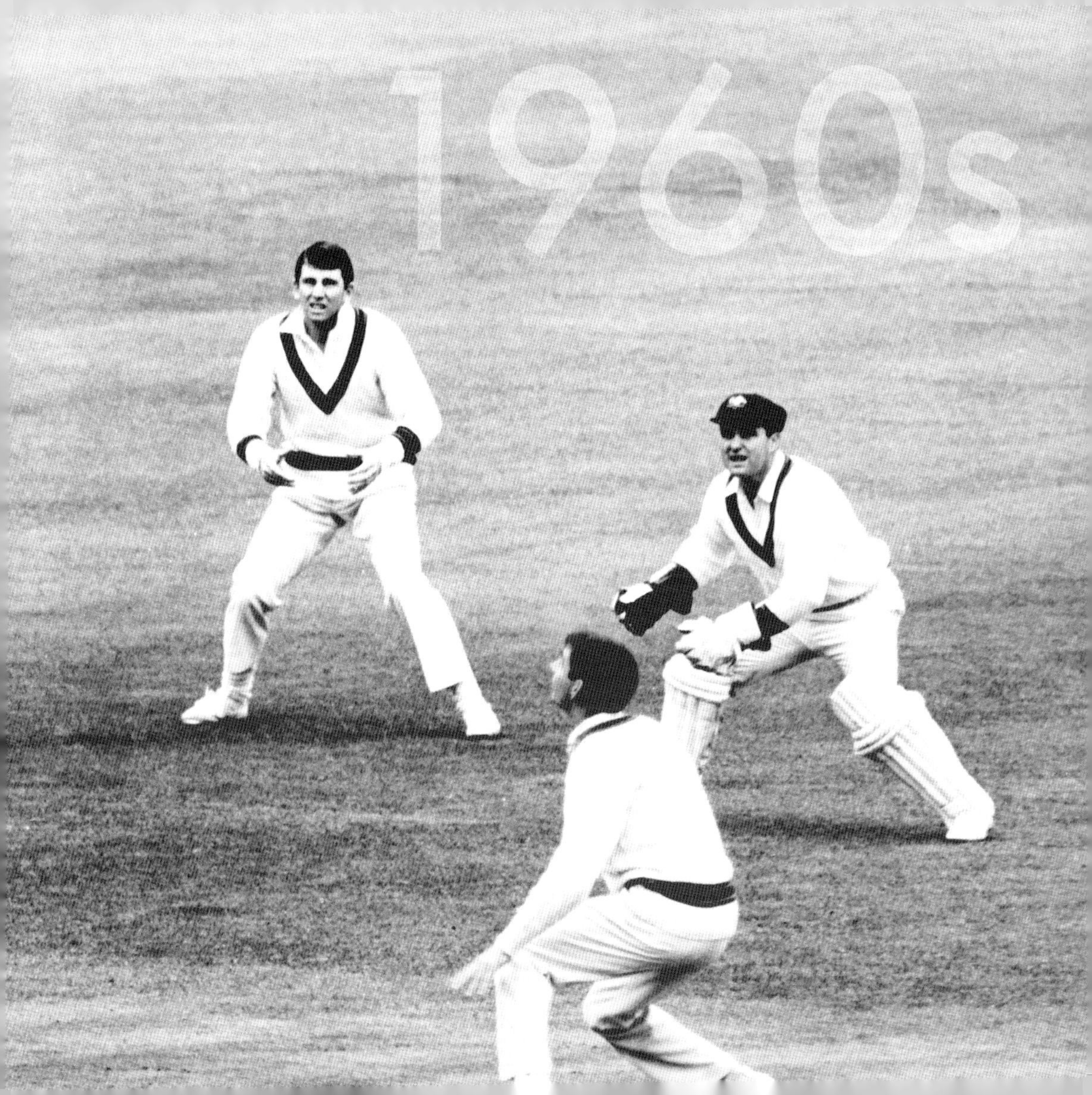
1960s

Previous spread: Geoff Boycott is caught Redpath bowled Connolly for 13 for the MCC against Australia at Lord's in 1964 on the third and final day of their three day match, which ended in a draw after rain interrupted proceedings.

Right: The members of the 1960 South African team alight their South African Airways plane on arrival at London Airport for their tour of England. They were met by small crowds of anti-apartheid demonstrators, but there were a strong police presence against any trouble.

Below: Riot halt the second Test between the West Indies and the MCC on 5 February 1960 at Port Of Spain. Because of a run-out decision by the Chinese umpire which brought about the dismissal of Charran Singh, a riot broke out amongst the indignant spectators and bottle throwing and swearing commenced. This picture shows Ted Dexter (the English captain) who appealed for the dismissal being escorted from the Queen's Oval pitch. In the background can be seen some of the bottles that had been thrown.

Left: The Australian Cricket team in
New Zealand 1960. Back Row (left to right):
B.C. Booth, B. Fisher, J.H. Shaw, J. Potter.
Middle Row: F.M. Misson, I.W. Quick,
J.C. Lill, G. Thomas, K.N. Slater. Front Row:
H.C. Smith (Manager), R.A. Gaunt,
R.B. Simpson, I.D. Craig (Captain),
L.V. Maddocks (Vice-Captain), J.W. Martin.

Below: Godfrey Evans in action for the
Duke of Norfolk's Eleven against the South
Africans at Arundel Castle in April 1960 –
a one day match which opened the tour.
Evans hits a four with this stroke, his first ball,
off Hugh Tayfield, while the wicket-keeper is
C. Duckworth.

Right: South Africa's Tony Pithy is caught Parks bowled Statham for 7 at Old Trafford on the fourth day of the fourth Test at Old Trafford in July 1960. With England already leading the Test series 3-0, this match and the subsequent fifth Test were both drawn.

Left: England lost two quick wickets in the last half-hour of play at Trent Bridge on the opening day in the third Test. Here is the first of them to go, Ray Illingworth caught and bowled by Tayfield for 37, after a valuable stand with Barrington which had yielded 75 runs. England would total 287 in their first innings before sensationally dismissing the tourists for 88 (Trueman 5-27) and 247 (Trueman 4-77). England reached the modest chase of 49 for the loss of 2 wickets.

Left: West Indian opener Conrad Hunte scores off Australian fast bowler Frank Misson at the WACA in November.

Above: Conrad Hunte is laden with gear as he leaves a train in Melbourne after a trip from Adelaide.

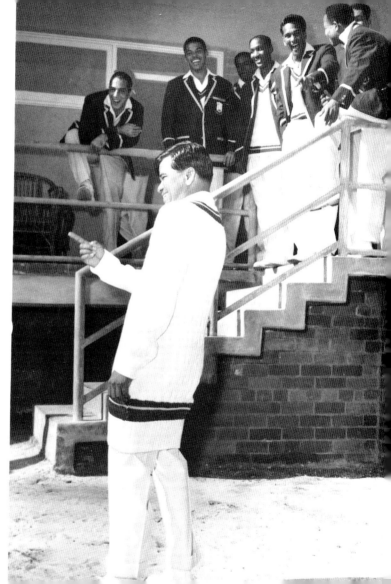

Above: The brilliant Garry Sobers off-drives Australia's Richie Benaud for four.

Left: Seymour Nurse, the young Barbados batsman at practice at the Brisbane Cricket Ground for the upcoming match against Queensland. Nurse, who was in line as a middle order batsman for the opening Test, would miss selection. He would however fight his way back into the team for the second Test.

Right: West Indies players celebrate running out Ian Meckiff to sensationally tie the first Test of the series at Woolloongabba, Brisbane, 14 December 1960.

Right: Lance Gibbs, the West Indian right-arm off-break bowler, played 79 Tests from 1958 until 1976 taking 309 wickets at an average of 29.09, in a highly decorated career.

Far left: Sonny Ramadhin in practice at the SCG No.2 nets in preparation for a Test match against Australia. After debuting for the West Indies in the first Test of the 1950 series against England, he would play his 43rd and final Test against Australia in the second Test of the 1960-61 series. A right-arm offbreak bowler, he took 158 wickets at 28.98.

Left: Looking grimly determined Richie Benaud, the New South Wales and Australian captain, led the Australians in the brilliant series against the West Indies during the summer of 1960-61 in Australia.

Left: The scene at the wicket at Adelaide Oval on the Saturday as Eric Freeman's six soars through the air on its way through the Victor Richardson Memorial Gates and into the street outside. The six pairs of eyes watching the balls flight, belong to Freeman, wicket-keeper Jackie Hendricks, Garry Sobers (right background), bowler Lance Gibbs, umpire Col Egar and batsman.

Below: Lance Gibbs signs autographs for admiring young Adelaide enthusiasts after his hat-trick against Australia in the drawn fourth Test.

Left: Ten members of the Australian cricket team leave Sydney for Melbourne for a three-day match in Launceston in March 1961, before heading on to England. Walking to the plane at Kingsford Smith Airport are (left to right): Bobby Simpson, Brian Booth, Neil Harvey, Frank Misson and captain Richie Benaud.

Right: All-rounder Ken Mackay of Queensland, who was a member of the 1961 Australian team to England.

Below: Vice-captain of the Australian tourists, Neil Harvey in England in April 1961.

Left: Neil Harvey leads out the Australians on the 1961 Ashes tour to England.

Below: Captain Richie Benaud presents Queen Elizabeth to the Australian team.

Left: Bad luck for England as the ball trickles onto Ted Dexter's wicket, bowled by Graham McKenzie for 17 runs in the second innings of the second Test at Lord's. With a first innings deficit of 134, England crashed to 4-80 in the afternoon session before being eventually dismissed for 202, leaving Australia requiring just 69 for victory. Despite some hostile bowling from England's Statham and Trueman Australia reached their modest target at five wickets down to take a 1-0 series lead.

Right: Australia's Peter Burge hits the winning stroke for Australia in the second Test. He remained at 37 not out from Australia's total of 5-71.

Above: Colin Cowdrey is caught Grout off McKenzie for 93 during England's first innings in the third Test at Headingly.

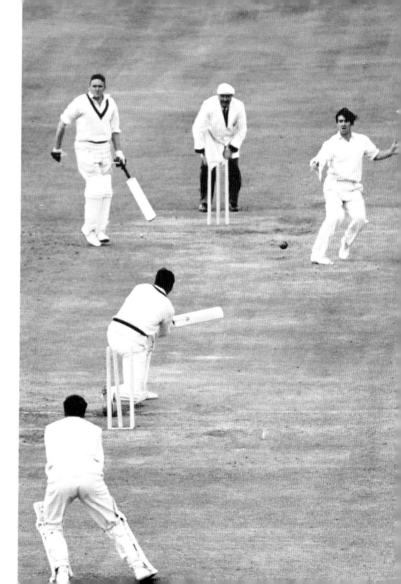

Right: Third Test hero Freddie Trueman clean bowls the Australian captain, Richie Benaud for a duck in the second innings (similar result in the first innings) as Trueman rips through the tourists batting line-up, taking 6-30. Requiring just 59 for victory, England would win by 8 wickets to level the series at 1-1 with two Tests remaining.

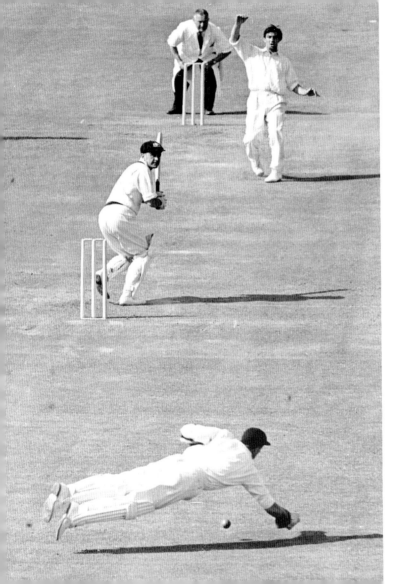

Left: Third Test action as Ken Mackay turns a ball from Trueman and wicket-keeper Murray makes a full length dive. Trueman pauses with arm raised as he watches from the far end.

Right: A few balls later Ken Mackay is caught Murray off Trueman for a duck as Australia crash to be all out in their second innings for 120.

Left: Australia wins fourth Test to retain Ashes. Freddie Trueman is caught by Benaud off Simpson for 8 in England's disastrous second innings on the last day. England collapsed from 1-150, to be all out for 201, giving Australia victory by 54 runs with just 20 minutes to spare.

Above: Peter Burge is caught by wicketkeeper J.T. Murray off Ted Dexter for 23 during Australia's second innings. With Burge's wicket Australia were 4-274 with an overall lead of just 97 after trailing by 177 on the first innings.

Right: Australian captain Richie Benaud, who walked to the wicket to a great ovation from the crowd, in what was almost certainly his last Test match in England, is bowled by Allen for 6 in Australia's first innings. Allen toiled admirably for England to take 4-133 from 30 overs.

Left: England skipper Peter May is out to Benaud for a duck, during the final day of the thrilling fourth Test. Benaud bowled his side to victory taking 6-70 to deny England what looked a certain victory.

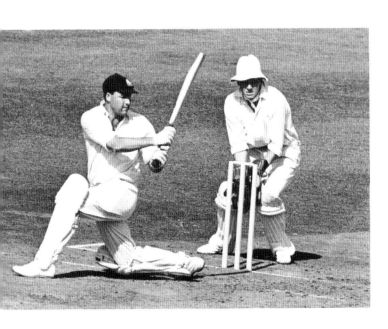

Above: Peter Burge sweeps a ball from R.G. Marler in the Australians match against Gentleman of England at Lord's (A.C. Smith is wicket-keeper), in one of four matches the tourists played after the final Test. Burge was eventually out for 74 to Marlar, who captured 6-184 from 59.5 overs!

Right: Fifth Test, second day as England wicket-keeper Murray makes a fine acrobatic save to stop runs off Norm O'Neill's bat in the Australian first innings. O'Neill would go on to score 117 runs (his highest score in the series) out of his sides 494 runs, which gave Australia a 238 run lead on the first innings.

Left: Rohan Kanhai cover drives Johnny Martin during his innings of 81 for Western Australia against NSW in late November.

Below: West Indian batsman Rohan Kanhai who played for Western Australia in the summer of 1961-62 receives a word of sympathy from the Governor-General after injuring a finger at the SCG against New South Wales in a Sheffield Shield contest. In seven matches in that summar Kanhai totalled 490 runs at an average of 44.18.

Right: West Indian Test star Wes Hall grins broadly as he plays an unorthodox stroke while playing for Queensland against NSW, to an awkward ball from spinner Johnny Martin, in the Shield match at the SCG. Fast-bowler Hall played 8 Shield matches that summer and was the leading wicket-taker in the overall competition with 43, and was almost a one-man band for his state, with B. Fisher next with just 19 wickets.

Left: A fine action picture of England's right-arm fast bowler David Larter during the fifth and final Test match against Pakistan at The Oval. On debut he captured 5-57 and 4-88 to help England to a 10 wicket win and a 4-0 win in the series.

Above: In August, Hanif Mohammed makes a spectacular catch to dismiss Colin Cowdrey off the bowling of Fazal Mahmood for 182 during England's first innings against Pakistan in the fifth Test at The Oval.

Left: England skipper Ted Dexter slams a ball from Fazal Mahmood during his century-making innings during the fifth Test against Pakistan. At stumps on the opening day he was 144 not out, and was eventually dismissed the next day for 172.

Right: The MCC touring team in Australia 1962-63. In no particular order: E.R. Dexter (Captain), M.C. Cowdrey (Vice-Captain), D.A. Allen, K.F. Barrington, L.J. Coldwell, T.W. Graveney, R. Illingworth, B.R. Knight, J.D.F. Larter, J.T. Murray, P.H. Parfitt, G. Pullar, D.S. Sheppard, A.C. Smith, J.B. Statham, F.J. Titmus, F.S. Trueman.

Right: Pakistan's innings come to a close as Intikhab Alam is clean bowled by Larter for 12, leaving England just 27 runs to win the Test, which they would do without loss.

Left: A life for Bobby Simpson in the Brisbane Test match. On the first day of the opening Test between Australia and England, Alan Smith, the England wicket-keeper dives for a catch offered by Bobby Simpson, but the ball fell clear. Simpson would go on to make 50 in Australia's first innings total of 404. England would reply with 389 before Australia would declare in their second innings setting England 378 to win. The match ended in a draw with England 6-278.

Left: Bobby Simpson looks around to see his middle stump lying some distance away after a fast and accurately placed ball from England's Trueman (bottom) during the first day of the second Test at Melbourne. Simpson had made 38 after an opening stand with Bill Lawry of 62.

Right: On the fifth day of the second Test England's David Sheppard just makes his crease as Barry Jarman whips off the bails after a smart return from the outfield from Peter Burge. Sheppard didn't learn his lesson from this close shave running between the wickets, eventually run out for 113.

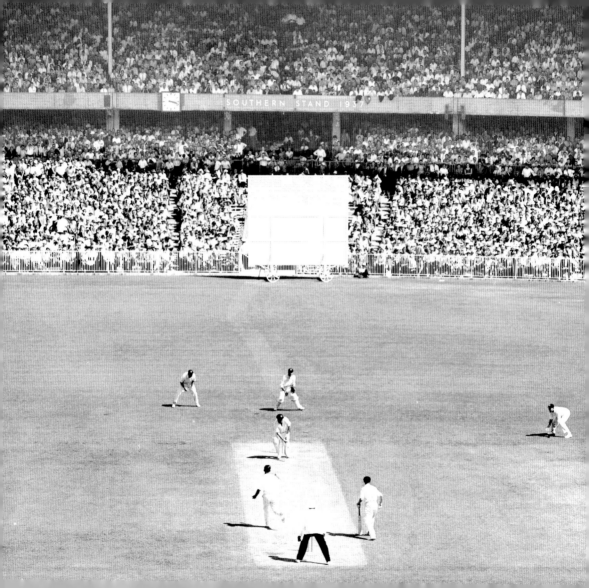

Right: Colin Cowdrey (bottom) and Ken Barrington force their way through an applauding crowd at Melbourne after England won the second Test. Immediately behind Barrington is Australia captain Richie Benaud followed by his Australian team-mates.

Left: Nearly 70,000 spectators attended the opening day's play in Melbourne for the second Test. Australia's middle order batsman Brian Booth defensively pushes a delivery from England spinner Freddie Titmus to square-leg. Titmus would get his man shortly after for 27, but Booth would get his revenge in the second innings, scoring 103.

Left: Young and not so young spectators rush onto the pitch to congratulate England cricketers after their seven wicket victory over Australia in the second Test. After England led by just 15 on the first innings, Freddie Trueman (5-62), supported by Brain Statham and Ted Dexter, tore the heart out of the Australian second innings, dismissing them for 248. Requiring 234 runs for victory, England safely reached their target for the loss of just three wickets.

Below: At the Sydney Cricket Ground England vice-captain Colin Cowdrey late-cuts a ball from a bowling machine invented by Australian engineer J.L. Black and used by the England team in final practice for the third Test. Similar machines had been used for tennis and golf, and baseball pitching was next on the list.

Left: Australian Prime Minister Menzies at Manuka Oval, Canberra with captains, Ted Dexter and Donald Bradman for the Prime Ministers XI and the MCC tour clash in February 1963.

Right: A ring of fielders crouch close to the bat as Australian Graham McKenzie bowls to England's injured John Murray towards the end of England's disastrous second innings of 104 in the third Test at the SCG. Fast bowlers Davidson (5-25) and McKenzie (3-26) did most of the damage as Australia levelled the series at 1-1 going to Adelaide.

Above: *England's Ken Barrington edges a ball from McKenzie past Simpson and Benaud for four during the first innings of the fourth Test* at Adelaide. He eventually made 63 before he was bowled by Simpson. Australia would set England 356 to win the match. They reached 4-223 with Barrington 132 not out as the match finished in a draw. The series would finish 1-1 with the fifth Test also drawn.

Above: A premature end to the third Test at Sydney as excited schoolchildren surged onto the pitch before the winning stroke had been hit by the Australian batsmen. The police had some difficulty in clearing the pitch before the game could be resumed for the winning stroke to be made. One umpire is seen protecting the stumps while at the other end the excited youngsters have already uprooted the wicket in a premature rush for souvenirs. England fieldsmen Barrington and Cowdrey look on.

Left: England middle-order batsman Ray Illingworth is hit by Australian fast bowler Alan Davidson during the fifth Test in February 1963 at the SCG.

Below: Members of the West Indian cricket touring team arrive in London at Paddington Station to start their tour of Britain on 8 April 1963. Frank Worrell (right) the West Indies captain, welcomes Mr Gaskin (left) the team manager and wicket-keeper David Allen (centre).

Right: Sir Garfield Sobers in April 1963. He debuted for the West Indies nine years earlier as a 17-year-old in 1954, and would play until 1974. He scored 8032 runs at 57.78 with 26 centuries and a high score of 365 not out against Pakistan in the third Test at Sabina Park in 1958. A left-arm bowler, he captured 235 wickets at 34.03 with a career best of 6-73, while also taking 109 catches. He remains one of the greatest cricketers the world has ever seen.

Right: It's October 1963 at the WACA Ground in Perth and South Africa has arrived for their tour of Australia, with Peter Carlstein, a top order batsman having some batting practice in the nets.

Left: West Indian wicket-keeper Deryck Murray attempts to stump Barry Knight off the bowling of Garry Sobers during the traditional one-day match at Arundel between the West Indies and The Duke of Norfolk's XI. Soon after this attempt, Murray was successful and had Knight out stumped off the bowling of Sobers.

Above: Australia's No 3 batsman Norman O'Neill starts his walk back to the dressing room after Peter Pollock (left) clean-bowled him for 21 in the first innings of the fifth Test in Sydney. With this match drawn the series remained level at 1-1.

Above: The Australian XI who played against South Africa at Melbourne from 15-19 November 1963. After South Africa trailed on the first innings by 108, some excellent bowling in the second innings by Seymour and Barlow, followed up with an Eddie Barlow century got the tourists home by 3 wickets.

Right: The bowling action of Queensland's Tom Veivers in England.

Left: The Australian Test team which was selected to tour England in 1964. Assembled together for their first game against a Tasmanian XI in Hobart in April. The squad was, back row (left to right): Arthur James (masseur), Neil Hawke, Graham Corling, Johnny Martin, Bob Cowper, Alan Connolly, D. Sherwood (scorer and baggage handler). Middle row: Rex Sellers, Tom Veivers, Jack Potter, Jack Ledward (assistant manager), Graham McKenzie, Ian Redpath, Barry Jarman. Front row: Peter Burge, Norman O'Neill, Bobby Simpson (captain), Ray Steele (manager), Brian Booth (vice-captain), Bill Lawry, Wally Grout.

Right: An elegant stroke from New South Wales batsman Brian Booth, a right-handed batsman who had established himself as Australia's most consistent scorer in the two series before the tour to England in 1964. In the previous 11 Tests he had played, Booth had reached 1,000 runs and scored four of Australia's eight Test centuries in the last two home series against England and South Africa. Tall and slender, he made his debut in first-class cricket in 1954/55 and in his second match scored an unbeaten 74 when NSW defeated MCC. Booth did not establish himself in Test cricket until he took part in Australia's victory at Old Trafford that retained the Ashes in 1961. In the 1964 series against England, Booth managed just 38 runs from 6 innings in the opening three Tests, before hitting form with 98 and 74 in the fourth and fifth Tests.

Left: Bill Lawry has some batting practice at Lord's on 20 April 1964.

Right: Ian Redpath, a newcomer to England has some batting practice at Lord's also on 20 April.

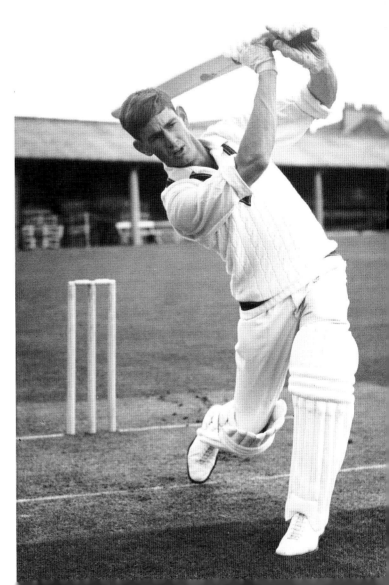

Left: Australia's Brian Booth (left) misses a chance from Geoff Boycott off a ball from Neil Hawke during England's first innings against Australia in the first Test at Trent Bridge, Nottingham. Boycott would eventually top-score with 48 from England's total of 8 (dec) for 216.

Above: England batsman Ken Barrington hooks a ball from Graham McKenzie on the second day of the first Test. The wicket-keeper is Wally Grout and next to him is Bobby Simpson. Barrington would be dismissed a short time later for 22 in England's first innings.

Left: Australia's Peter Burge is out lbw to Freddie Trueman for 31 in Australia's first innings of 168 in the first Test. The other batsman is skipper Bobby Simpson.

Left: Australia's top order batsman Norm O'Neill attempts to cover drive Freddie Trueman during the second Test at Lord's. In a low scoring match O'Neill would score 26 and 22 in respective innings out of totals of just 176 and 4-168. The opening two Tests had both finished in disappointing draws.

Below: England's Peter Parfitt, who was injured in the first innings of the third Test, drives a ball from Australia's Tom Veivers for 4 runs. Parfitt would be out shortly after for 6 runs as England were dismissed for 229, leaving Australia the simple task of chasing 109 for victory, which they duly did to take a 1-0 lead in the five Test series.

Left: The end for Bobby Simpson as the Australian skipper walks away from his crease after being caught behind the wicket by wicketkeeper Jim Parks, but not before hitting the highest score to-date at Old Trafford, scoring 311. Other players in the picture are (bottom left) bowler Price, and (top left) Fred Rumsey. In another drawn Test, Australia declared at 8-656 before England responded with 611 all out.

Below: England bowler Freddie Trueman moves towards 300 Test wickets. In the fifth Test Trueman took wickets off consecutive balls just before lunch against Australia at The Oval to have him on 299 wickets. After being dropped for the fourth Test at Old Trafford bowled right-handed batsman Ian Redpath then with the next ball he had

Graham McKenzie caught in the slips by Colin Cowdrey. A jubilant Cowdrey is pictured after he caught out McKenzie. Trueman would eventually get his 300th wicket shortly later when he finished off the Australian innings with the wickets of Hawke and Corling.

Left: Australian Barry Jarman just reaches his crease for a quick single as wicket-keeper M.G. Griffith stretches for the ball in the President's XI v Australia match at Lord's after the fifth Test.

Above: In November 1964 former Australian Test captain Lindsay Hassett discovered the fervent women cricketers of Noumea are hard to beat. The women wore uniforms of voluminous ankle-length 'Mother Hubbards' in all colours of the rainbow. And what they lacked in orthodox play they made up for in enthusiasm. They played 17 to a side, use rubber balls and home-made bats longer and thinner than the standard Test bat. The whole experience is like a carnival, with lots of barracking and after a day of cricket they get together and do a kind of New Zealand haka.

Above: The New Zealand cricketers arrive at London airport in England for their tour in April 1965. They had just completed seven Tests: losing 1-0 to India in four Tests, and also lost 2-0 to Pakistan in three Tests.

Left: Benaud the director! Former Australian Test captain, Richie Benaud, who is directing a film on cricket coaching, stands over the camera crew at Albert Cricket Ground, in Melbourne, Australia in February 1965. Bob Cowper is batting at the other end. Other stars in the film were Sir Donald Bradman, Peter Burge, Wally Grout, Alan Davidson, Graham McKenzie and Barry Jarman. The film was not shown commercially, but instead exhibited at schools.

Above: England skipper Mike Smith congratulates Trevor Goddard on reaching his century (his first in Test cricket), during the fourth Test between South Africa and England at Johannesburg in January 1965. England won the series 1-0, with the only result in the first Test at Durban in early December, when the tourists won by an innings and 104 runs.

Right: Wes Hall playing in Australia in the 1960's, was part of the West Indies team that took on and defeated the Australians in a five match Test series 2-1 at home from March to May, 1965. Hall captured 16 wickets in this series for the Windies at 28.37, second only to Lance Gibbs who took 18 at 30.89

Left: The skipper of the New Zealand touring party J.R. Reid putting on pads watched by four of the team, when they visited Surridge's Sports Shop in London the day after arriving on 24 April. Watching are (left to right) G.E. Vivian, V.T. Pollard, J.T. Ward and B. Taylor. Later that day they played at The Oval against the London New Zealand cricket club.

Below: All eyes are on Kiwi Bevan Congdon (second from right), who juggles a catch from England opener Bob Barber during the first Test at Edgbaston. Players are (from left to right) Barber, wicket-keeper A.E. Dick and skipper John Reid at first slip.

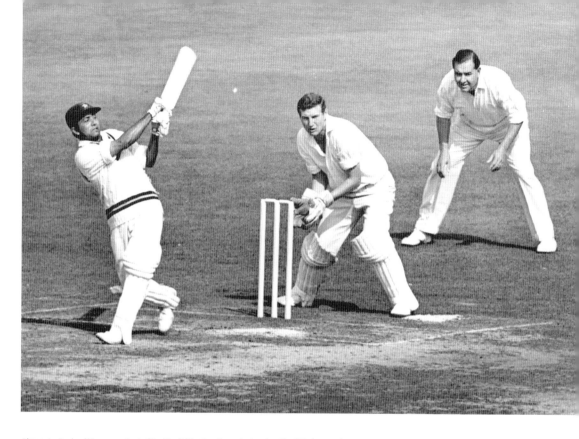

Above: An England XI versus a Rest of the World XI at Lord's on the last day. Hanif Mohammed (Pakistan Rest of World), hits out to a ball from R.W. Barber, with the wicket-keeper Jim Parks and Colin Cowdrey at first slip.

Left: BBC-TV cameramen dressed in clothing protecting them from the freezing conditions during the first Test.

Right: The attendance on the second day was kept to a minimum with a cold wind and cloudy skies. Here is a view showing the deserted stands.

Below: New Zealand fielders and umpires W.S. Price and C.S. Elliott enjoying hot tea on the ground during the second day. Tea was taken out by England twelfth man David Allen (holding teapot). In the centre is England batsman Colin Cowdrey (with cap), with his team-mate Ken Barrington to his left.

Left: After England totalled 435 in their first innings, New Zealand batsmen struggled in reply, being bowled out for just 116. Middle order batsman Bert Sutcliffe was forced to retire hurt, as he puts a hand up to his ear after being struck by a Freddie Trueman bouncer.

Above: The New Zealand batsmen were really in the wars against a fired up England attack. In this picture opening batsman Bevan Congdon puts his handkerchief up to his mouth as he is helped off the Edgbaston pitch by England skipper Mike Smith (left) and the other opening batsman G.T. Dowling after being hit in the face following a ball from Bob Barber during the first innings.

Above: Bert Sutcliffe is also helped from the field by skipper Jim Reid. Sutcliffe tried to bat on but had to retire.

Left: The South African cricketers on their arrival at London Airport in June. In the front without hats are Peter van der Merwe (captain) and Eddie Barlow (vice-captain).

Below: South Africa's Eddie Barlow hits a ball for four against Essex at the Garrison Cricket Ground, Colchester. In a drawn match Barlow went on to score 78 in the first innings.

Below: South African tourist to England, Colin Bland, in 1965. A fine right-hand batsman and medium-paced bowler, who also excelled as a cover fieldsman.

Below: South African wicket-keeper Denis Lindsay shows his agility at training while on an earlier tour of Australia.

Left: Anti-apartheid slogans are being held by demonstrators, who are watched by police, outside The Oval Cricket Ground in Kennington, London, where the all-white South African team were playing Surrey in a three day game.

Right: An action picture of the South African fast bowler Peter Pollock playing at Trent Bridge in the second Test against England. Pollock's bowling was the major reason for his team's win in this match by 94 runs, capturing 5-53 in the first innings and 5-34 in the second.

Above: Captain of the 1965 South African tourists to England, Peter van der Merwe.

Above: Another South African tourist, Ali Bacher.

Above: New Zealand fielder B.R. Taylor dives through the air in an unsuccessful attempt to get a catch off P.H. Parfitt of England during the third Test. Parfitt would be finally dismissed for 32 in England's first innings of 4 (dec) for 546, in which Edrich (310) and Barrington (163) would put on 369 for the second wicket.

Right: Ken Barrington is caught by New Zealand wicket-keeper J.T. Ward off R.C. Motz for 163. England would go on and win this third Test by an innings and 187 to register a 3-0 series win.

Below: The Pollock brothers, Graeme (left) and Peter at The Oval in preparation for the final Test against England. The Pollocks were standout performers during the series, with fast-bowler Peter the leading wicket-taker with 20 at just 18.30, while batsman Graeme was top scorer with 291 runs at 48.50.

Above: England "night watchman" D.J. Brown is caught at second slip by R. Dumbrill, bowled McKinnon for a duck during England's first innings. The wicket-keeper is D. Lindsay and at first slip is E. Barlow. Match scores were: South Africa 208 and 392, and England 202 and 4-308.

Right: J.R. Reid is out lbw to Ray Illingworth for 54, which was top-score in his team's first innings total of 193 in the third Test. Illingworth finished with 4-42.

Above: Wally Grout and Bobby Simpson dive but can't reach a ball hit by England's Ken Barrington off Hawke during England's first innings of the fourth Test. Barrington was the most successful English batsman with scores of 60 and 102.

Left: Peter Burge played his final Test series in the summer of 1965-66 against England. After debuting for Australia in 1955, he played in 42 Tests and scored 2290 runs at 38.16 with a high score of 181. A Queenslander, he also held his states individual record score of 283 v NSW in 1963-64 at the time.

Left: Bill Lawry congratulates Bob Simpson on his 100 during Australia's first innings of the fourth Test. Simpson went on to score 225, the highest score by an Australian at Adelaide against England. Sir Donald Bradman held the previous record of 212 set in 1937. Australia struck back to win the fourth Test at Adelaide to level the series at 1-1. England, who batted first on the placid Adelaide wicket, collapsed and we're all out for 241. Spearhead of the Australia attack was fast bowler McKenzie who took six wickets for 48 runs. In Australia's first innings the openers Simpson and Lawry created a new first wicket partnership record of 244 before Lawry was out for 119. This beat the previous record of 201, also set by Simpson and Lawry, at Manchester in 1964. Simpson went on to score 225 out of Australia's first innings total of 516. England's second innings began badly and by stumps on the fourth day had already lost Barber, Boycott and Edrich for only 64 runs. Next day Australia forced home its advantage to have England all out for 266 for a win by an innings and nine runs. Barrington (102) and Titmus (53) provided the only resistance to the Australian bowling which was headed this time by Hawke who finished the innings with 5-54.

Right: A celebratory smile from young Australian cricketer Doug Walters after scoring a century (155) in his Test debut against England in the first Test in Brisbane. Being forced to follow-on, 163 runs in arrears on the first innings, England reached 3-186 to hold out for a draw.

Below: Australian opener Bill Lawry presents a broad bat to a David Brown delivery at the start of Australia's first innings in the fifth Test.

SOUTHERN STAND

Left: English fast bowler Jeff Jones stands open-mouthed as Graham Thomas hooks him to the boundary in the early stages of Australia's first innings. Jones would eventually get his man for just 19 to have Australia in early trouble at 2-36. Bill Lawry is the other batsman.

Below: A near thing for Bill Lawry as he is beaten by a ball from Jeff Jones. Captain Bob Simpson is the other batsman.

Right: Bob Cowper hooks one to the boundary during his record-breaking innings of 307. England and Australia went on run-scoring sprees in the fifth Test at the MCG. Mike Smith declared the England innings closed at 9 (dec) for 485. Australia started their reply shakily losing Simpson and then Thomas to be at 2-36, before Bob Cowper strode to the crease to change the complexion of the Test. A 212 third wicket stand with Lawry (108), followed by a 172 fourth wicket stand with Walters (60) had Australia safe from the possibility of defeat. Simpson would also declare the innings at 8-543. England would bat out the remainder of the final day to finish at 3-69 with the match drawn and the series squared at 1-1.

Right: MCC cricketers arrive at London Airport in March 1966, on return from Australia, looking tanned by the Antipodean sun. From left to right are: Colin Cowdrey, Billy Griffiths (tour manager), Mike Smith, Ken Higgs, David Brown and Geoff Boycott.

Below: West Indian Charlie Griffith bowls to Colin Milburn who ducks to avoid a bouncer in the MCC v West Indies tour match in May at Lord's.

Right: Australian fast bowler Neil Hawke, who shared the bowling honours in the series against England with Graham McKenzie, each capturing 16 wickets, with Hawke's 5-54 in the second innings of the fourth Test instrumental in Australia's victory.

Right: The large crowd at Lord's during the England v West Indies second Test of the 1966 series.

Above: A line of spectators hold newspapers over their heads to keep off the heavy rain, during the first day's play of the second Test. There would be no result in this match, before the Windies would win both the third and fourth Tests with England gaining some consolation with a win in the final Test.

Right: England Test cricketers Basil D'Oliveira and Tom Graveney practice at Lord's for the upcoming second Test against the West Indies, which started the next day. After the tourists had won the opening Test by an innings and 40 runs the home side needed a quick reply after spinner Lance Gibbs had destroyed the English batting in both innings with returns of 5-37 and then 5-69.

Above: Players shoot it out for the right to nominate a charity for a £50 cheque put up by the Rank Organisation to mark the opening of their Hotel Division's new Bridgford Hotel at Trent Bridge, Nottingham. The winner by the way was Ken Barrington, who donated the amount to the Nottinghamshire Old Peoples' Welfare Committee. Picture shows, left to right: Colin Milburn (Northants and England); Ken Barrington (Surrey and England); David Allan (West Indies) and Rudolf Cohen (West Indies).

Left: December 1966 saw the demolition of the Tavern and Clock Tower boxes at Lord's, to be replaced by the new stand.

Below: An umbrella field as Ken Cunningham plays forward at a ball from Jim Hubble, during Favell's XI second innings against Australia in a bushfire relief "Test" at Melbourne in April 1967. Brian Taber is the wicket-keeper and at first slip is Bobby Simpson. The match was held in aid of Tasmania bushfire victims.

Left: The Indian cricket team arrive at Heathrow Airport in April for their British tour in 1967.

Below: Members of the Indian cricket team, led by their captain, the Nawab of Pataudi (holding ball and cap) walk across the Lord's pitch on their way to their first practice session in the nets in late April.

Above: England captain Brian Close calls for three cheers for H.M. The Queen (standing on Pavillion steps) after H.M. had met the teams on the fourth day of the second Test. England would wrap up the match early on day four by an innings and 124 run win to take a 2-0 lead in the three match series.

Left: The Lord's Taverners hold a luncheon at the Café Royal, Regents Street, London to welcome the Indian touring team of 1967. The Nawab of Pataudi, the captain of the squad is with English comedian Harry Secombe.

Above: Pakistan batsman Saeed Ahmed drives a ball from England's Derek Underwood to the offside and takes a single during his fine second innings at Trent Bridge in the second Test. Saeed played a lone hand, scoring 68 out of his team's dismal total of 114.

Underwood destroyed the Pakistan second innings, finishing with 5-52 to set up an England win by 10 wickets. Also in the picture are England fieldsmen, Graveney (far Left), captain Close (second left), Cowdrey (third from left) and wicket-keeper Knott (partially hidden by Saed).

Above: South African Eddie Barlow, playing for a Rest of the World XI against Pakistan at Lord's in September. He has been clean bowled by Salim Altaf for a duck.

Left: Three Surrey players selected for the MCC team to tour the West Indies in the English winter, photographed in August 1967. They are left to right: Ken Barrington, John Edrich and Pat Pocock.

Left: A view style of watching cricket at the WACA Ground in Perth, Western Australia 1967.

Right: All first class matches in Western Australia are still played at the Western Australia Cricket Association Ground in Perth, the capital. With gentle sloping hills all you had to do was find a patch of grass for yourself with maybe an Esky or possibly park the pram, or if you wanted a seat, find a spot of the wooden seats around near the playing perimeter.

Left: Crowds of schoolboys invade the field to mob Bill Lawry and Bob Simpson after both had completed centuries during the second Test against India at Melbourne. Lawry was first out for exactly 100, while Simpson made 109 as the Australian openers put on 191 for the opening wicket.

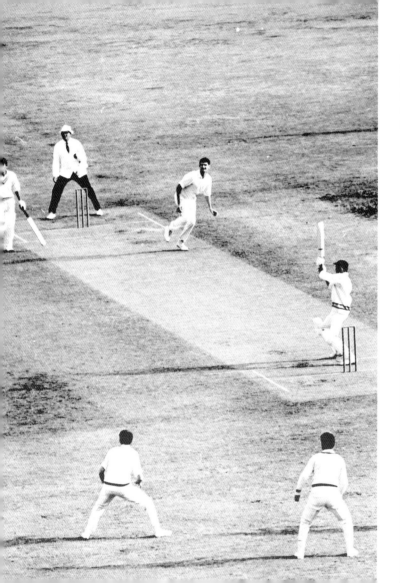

Left: Indian batsman Surti, who retired injured early on the opening day, returned later in the afternoon session to resume his innings, before he was eventually dismissed for 30, lbw to Simpson. India finished the day at 8-156.

Right: The Nawab of Pataudi, hampered by his injured left leg, awkwardly returned this ball from Graham McKenzie during the Indian second innings.

Below: Australian fast bowler Dave Renneberg leaps in frustration as wicket-keeper Barry Jarman (extreme right) and Australian captain Bob Simpson dive in vain from a shot by Indian Ajit Wadekar. For Wadekar, he would eventually be dismissed for 99 in the second innings.

Left: In March 1968 England surprisingly won the fourth Test courtesy of a bold West Indies declaration. England went to Guyana for the final Test holding a 1-0 series lead, which they would defend to take the series. Here Geoff Boycott, England opening batsman, cover drives West Indies fast-bowler David Holford for four during top-score 116 in their first innings. Behind the wicket is Deryck Murray while Rohan Kanhai is at slip. Rain stopped play early on day three, with England 1-146 in reply to West Indies 414 all out. England would eventually trail 43 on the first innings. The Windies would bat a second time and score 264, leaving England 308 to win. Despite brilliant bowling by both Gibbs (6-60) and Sobers (3-53) stumps would be drawn with England 9-206, with batsmen Alan Knott 73 from 260 balls and I. Jones 0 not out.

Above: It's April 1968 and Dave Renneberg carries plastic-protected suits over his shoulder as he arrives with Australian team-mates, left to right, Johnny Gleeson, Ian Chappell and Paul Sheahan, at Heathrow Airport to-day for their tour of Britain.

Above: Captain Bill Lawry gives some fielding practice at Lord's. Left to right are: Ian Redpath, Dave Renneberg, Les Joslin and Paul Sheahan.

Right: In May 1968 Garry Sobers turned film actor, and here he is with his name on the chair to prove it. The West Indies Test captain (also captain of Nottinghamshire at the time) is pictured at Westminster School cricket ground, Vincent Square, London, during the shooting of scenes for 'Two Gentleman Sharing.' For Sobers it was his first and only appearance in a feature film. He doubled for Hal Frederick, the coloured American actor who plays the part of a Jamaican and a cricket fanatic.

Right: The Australians practicing at the nets at Lord's, the day before the second Test.

Left: Ian Chappell having bowling practice.

Below left: Paul Sheahan gets in some batting practice.

Below centre: Ken Barrington batting in the nets in preparation for the 200th Test match between England and Australia starting in a few days.

Below: Paul Sheahan (background) and John Inverarity, surrounded by bats and some pads as a press conference is being held for the team at the Waldorf Hotel in London.

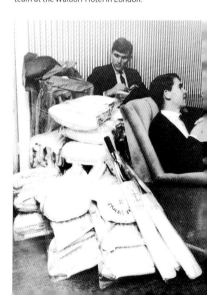

Above: The England team for the third Test against at Edgbaston. Back row (left to right): B.R. Knight, J.A. Snow, D.J. Brown, D.L. Underwood, J.H. Edrich, A.P. Knott, G. Boycott. Front row: K.F. Barrington, T.W. Graveney, M.C. Cowdrey, R. Illingworth.

Below: Opener John Edrich takes a single during his knock of 164 in England's first innings. The wicket-keeper is Barry Jarman.

The second Test between England and
Australia at Lord's, which was also the 200th
Test match between the two countries.
A general view of the match in progress,
while England are batting. The new Tavern
Stand and Pavilion is seen in the background.

Above: Australian slip fielder Ian Chappell (centre) misses a chance offered by England batsman Ted Dexter off Alan Connolly's bowling. Dexter would be later bowled by John Gleeson for 21.

Below: Australian captain Bill Lawry adopts a one-footed stance as he hits out at a ball from John Snow, during the team's first inning. Fielders are (left to right): Colin Milburn, captain Colin Cowdrey and Tom Graveney. Lawry's knock of 135 held the Australian innings together to reach 324, but stilled trailed by 170 on the first innings.

Right: Doug Walters looks a forlorn figure as he is caught by wicket-keeper Alan Knott bowled Dave brown for 5 leaving Australia at 4-161 in reply to England's 494 during Australia's first innings against England at The Oval.

Left: Ian Chappell is caught by wicket-keeper Alan Knott off Dave Brown for 10 during Australia's first innings. Captain Colin Cowdrey makes a loud appeal at first slip.

Right: Alan Connolly removes England opener Colin Milburn's middle stump for 8 to have England 1-28 in the first innings. Umpire Charlie Elliott doesn't need to take his hand out of his pocket to make a decision.

Below: Paul Sheahan is clean bowled by off-break bowler Ray Illingworth for 14 as Australia slump to 5-185, still 309 behind England's first innings total. Fielders are captain Colin Cowdrey and wicketkeeper Alan Knott.

Left: Ian Redpath cuts John Snow to the boundary during Australia's first innings. Lawry and Redpath put on 129 for the second wicket after opener Inverarity's early dismissal.

Above: Players stand in silence for one minute at The Oval, before the start of the fourth day's play in the final Test. They stood in tribute to the famous Australian batsman Stanley Joseph McCabe who died suddenly aged 58 in the garden of his home at Beauty Point on Sydney Harbour foreshore the day before.

Above: Wes Hall, playing for A Rest of the World XI against Australia at Lord's, sweeps a ball from Ian Chappell for one. Hall would remain 8 not out as The World side would be dismissed for 107 in their second innings leaving Australia 101 for victory, which they managed for the loss of two wickets.

Right: Tailender Ashley Mallett turns a delivery from Derek Underwood to the boundary during his valuable knock of 43 in Australia's first innings. England fielders Alan Knott and Basil D'Oliveira watch the progress of the ball.

Right: It's only a split second after the ball has snicked his bat, but already West Australian vice-captain John Inverarity must fear the worst. Wicketkeeper Jackie Hendricks is moving into position to take the catch which will leave the West Australian score at 2-12 in the second innings. The successful bowler is big Wes Hall, who captured three wickets in each innings as the tourists won by 6 wickets.

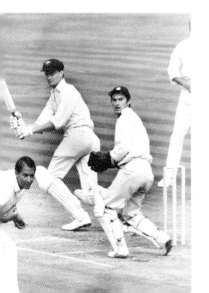

Left: Sir Donald Bradman raises the flag during the Australia Day ceremony at Adelaide Oval before play in the fourth Test in January 1969 as captains Sir Garfield Sobers and Bill Lawry stand to attention. In an exciting match the Australians batted first and scored 533, to hold a massive first innings lead of 257 (Windies scoring 276). Batting a second time the Windies attacked from the outset and scored heavily to reach 616, leaving Australia 360 to win. In an exciting finish, Australia looked headed for victory reaching 3-304, before some poor running between the wickets (4 run-outs) and good bowling had Australia at 9-339 when stumps were called to hold out for a draw.

Left: At the conclusion of the fifth Test at the Sydney Cricket Ground, the Frank Worrell trophy is presented by the West Indies skipper Garry Sobers to Australian captain Bill Lawry. Australia won the series 3-1 after clinching victory with a 382 run victory in the final Test.

Right: Opening batsman Roy Fredericks plays in typical cavalier West Indian style against England in the first Test at Old Trafford in June. England won the opening Test by 10 wickets with opener Geoffrey Boycott's first inning century (128) guiding his side to a commanding first innings lead when England's opening bowlers (John Snow and Dave Brown) tore through the tourists batting line-up. The Windies never recovered, though they made a better fist of their second innings. In the three Test series, the second Test was drawn and England won a close affair in the final match by 30 runs.

Below: South Australian Test batsman Ian Chappell is congratulated by his grandfather, former Test player Victor Richardson after being named cricketer of the year for the 1968-69 season. Chappell received the 'Golden Peanut' trophy from the Governor of NSW, Sir Roden Cutler during the week. The award was made annually by the Peanut Marketing Board of Kingaroy, Queensland.

Left: A welcome cup of tea for two New Zealand century makers, after the tourists declaration at The Oval in a tour match against Surrey. B.A.G. Murray (left), who scored 123 and V. Pollard (100 not out) relax by the changing rooms. In the Test series that year, England won the first Test by 230 runs. Match scores were: England 190 (R. Illingworth 53) and 340 (J.H. Edrich 115), New Zealand 169 (D.L. Underwood 4-38, R. Illingworth 4-37) and 131 (D.L. Underwood 7-32). The second Test was drawn New Zealand 294 (B.F. Hastings 83) and 1-66, England 451 (J.H. Edrich 155, P.J. Sharpe 111). England wrapped up the three match series by 8 wickets at The Oval. New Zealand 150 (D.L. Underwood 6-41) and 229 (D.L. Underwood 6-60) and England 242 (J.H. Edrich 68 and B.R. Taylor 4-47) and 2-138 (M.H. Denness 55 not out).

Right: South Australian and West Indian batsman Lance Gibbs is in full flight down the wicket but he is too late. Young Western Australia wicket-keeper Rodney Marsh already has the bails off and Gibbs is run out. During this period many West Indian cricketers played Sheffield Shield cricket in Australia and also County Cricket in England, much was their appeal as well as their various abilities.

Pakistan v Worcestershire, 1971.

1970S CRICKET TESTS:

SEASON	OPPONENTS	RESULT	No. TESTS
1970/71	THE ASHES (ENGLAND IN AUSTRALIA)	ENGLAND 2-0	7
	ENGLAND IN NEW ZEALAND	ENGLAND 1-0	2
	INDIA IN WEST INDIES	INDIA 1-0	5
1971	PAKISTAN IN ENGLAND	ENGLAND 1-0	3
	INDIA IN ENGLAND	INDIA 1-0	3
1971/72	NEW ZEALAND IN WEST INDIES	DRAWN 0-0	5
1972	THE ASHES (AUSTRALIA IN ENGLAND)	DRAWN 2-2	5
1972/73	PAKISTAN IN AUSTRALIA	AUSTRALIA 3-0	3
	ENGLAND IN INDIA	INDIA 2-1	5
	PAKISTAN IN NEW ZEALAND	PAKISTAN 1-0	3
	ENGLAND IN PAKISTAN	DRAWN 0-0	3
	THE FRANK WORRELL TROPHY (AUSTRALIA IN WEST INDIES)	AUSTRALIA 2-0	5
1973	NEW ZEALAND IN ENGLAND	ENGLAND 2-0	3
	THE WISDEN TROPHY (WEST INDIES IN ENGLAND)	WEST INDIES 2-0	3
1973/74	NEW ZEALAND IN AUSTRALIA	AUSTRALIA 2-0	3
	AUSTRALIA IN NEW ZEALAND	DRAWN 1-1	3
	THE WISDEN TROPHY (ENGLAND IN WEST INDIES)	DRAWN 1-1	5
1974	INDIA IN ENGLAND	ENGLAND 3-0	3
	PAKISTAN IN ENGLAND	DRAWN 0-0	3
1974/75	WEST INDIES IN INDIA	WEST INDIES 3-2	5
	THE ASHES (ENGLAND IN AUSTRALIA)	AUSTRALIA 4-1	6
1974/75	ENGLAND IN NEW ZEALAND	ENGLAND 1-0	2
	WEST INDIES IN PAKISTAN	DRAWN 0-0	2
1975	THE ASHES (AUSTRALIA IN ENGLAND)	AUSTRALIA 1-0	4
1975/76	THE FRANK WORRELL TROPHY (WEST INDIES IN AUSTRALIA)	AUSTRALIA 5-1	6
	INDIA IN NEW ZEALAND	DRAWN 1-1	3
	INDIA IN WEST INDIES	WEST INDIES 2-1	4

SEASON	OPPONENTS	RESULT	No. TESTS
1976	THE WISDEN TROPHY (WEST INDIES IN ENGLAND)	WEST INDIES 3-0	5
1976/77	NEW ZEALAND IN PAKISTAN	PAKISTAN 2-0	3
	NEW ZEALAND IN INDIA	INDIA 2-0	3
	PAKISTAN IN AUSTRALIA	DRAWN 1-1	3
	ENGLAND IN INDIA	ENGLAND 3-1	5
	AUSTRALIA IN NEW ZEALAND	AUSTRALIA 1-0	2
	CENTENARY TEST (ENGLAND IN AUSTRALIA)	AUSTRALIA 1-0	1
	PAKISTAN IN WEST INDIES	WEST INDIES 2-1	5
1977	THE ASHES (AUSTRALIA IN ENGLAND)	ENGLAND 3-0	5
1977/78	ENGLAND IN PAKISTAN	DRAWN 0-0	3
	INDIA IN AUSTRALIA	AUSTRALIA 3-2	5
	ENGLAND IN NEW ZEALAND	DRAWN 1-1	3
	THE FRANK WORRELL TROPHY (AUSTRALIA IN WEST INDIES)	WEST INDIES 3-1	5
1978	PAKISTAN IN ENGLAND	ENGLAND 2-0	3
	NEW ZEALAND IN ENGLAND	ENGLAND 3-0	3
1978/79	INDIA IN PAKISTAN	PAKISTAN 2-0	3
	WEST INDIES IN INDIA	INDIA 1-0	6
	THE ASHES (ENGLAND IN AUSTRALIA)	ENGLAND 5-1	6
	PAKISTAN IN NEW ZEALAND	PAKISTAN 1-0	3
	PAKISTAN IN AUSTRALIA	DRAWN 1-1	2
1979	INDIA IN ENGLAND	ENGLAND 1-0	4
1979/80	AUSTRALIA IN INDIA	INDIA 2-0	6
	ENGLAND IN AUSTRALIA	AUSTRALIA 3-0	3
	PAKISTAN IN INDIA	INDIA 2-0	6
	THE FRANK WORRELL TROPHY (WEST INDIES IN AUSTRALIA)	WEST INDIES 2-0	3

Left: Groundsmen placing barbed-wire into position to protect the playing area of a snow-covered pitch at The Oval, February 1970. Precautions were taken to prevent the pitch being damaged by anti-apartheid protestors before the proposed tour of South Africa that coming summer.

Right: Part of the MCC's plans to protect cricket grounds and pitches from anti-apartheid demonstrators during the summer of 1970s when South Africa toured England. Work on the cricket square, as seen through the barbed wire at The Oval.

Below: The defences go up at Lord's Cricket Ground in preparation for the expected protests against the coming tour of the South Africa Cricket team, 5 February 1970. Three hundred reels of barbed wire have already been fixed on the surrounding walls and gates.

Above: Rival captains Ray Illingworth (left)
and Garry Sobers prior to the England v
The Rest of the World match for the Guinness
Trophy, June 1970. In the first match, The
Rest of the World XI crushed England by an
innings and 80 runs. Both Illingworth and
Sobers, top-scored in their team's respective
innings. Illingworth made 63 (out of 127) and
94 (out of 339), while Sobers scored a brilliant
183 (out of 546).

Left: Following the decision to abandon the
highly controversial tour by South Africa on
23 May 1970, staff begin to remove barbed
wire from the famous Kensington Oval which
was installed to thwart any attempts by
anti-apartheid demonstrators to sabotage
the pitch.

Left: Supporters of the 'Stop the Seventy Tour' outside Lord's Cricket Ground, London, on 2 May 1970. Cricket fans were given a 'preview' of anti-apartheid demonstrations planned for the South African tour that summer.

Right: Anti-apartheid demonstrators in cricket gear stop traffic outside the Lord's Tavern next to the Grace Gates in 1970.

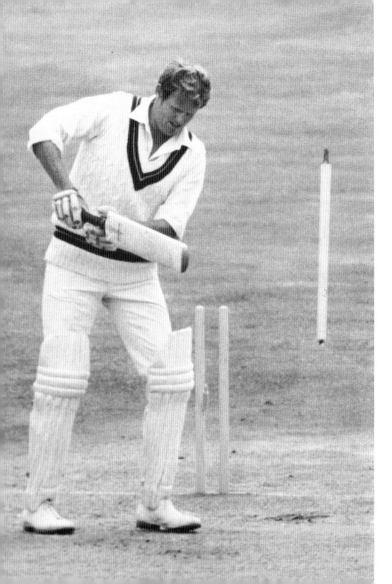

Left: Action from the fifth and final match in the series as a stump flies through the air as Graeme Pollock is bowled by Peter Lever during The Rest of the World's First Innings against England at The Oval, August 1970. Pollock scored 114 in the second innings to help set up The Rest of the World's 4 wicket victory, and seal a 4-1 series win.

Above: England representatives against The Rest of the World, from left, Colin Cowdrey and Ray Illingworth, July 1970. Both players were in line for the MCC captaincy for the upcoming tour of Australia, with Illingworth winning out over former captain Cowdrey.

Right: The MCC touring squad to Australia, 1970-71.

303

Left: The first Test of the 1970-71 Ashes series at Brisbane, December 1970. Ian Redpath is out, caught by MCC captain Ray Illingworth off the bowling of Derek Underwood during Australia's first innings total of 433. England replied with 464.

Above: Australia batsman Keith Stackpole looks for his 200th run in the first Test against England, December 1970 in Brisbane. Stackpole went on to score 207 in the match, which finished in a draw.

Above: Keith Fletcher (England) is bowled by part-time bowler Doug Walters in the second Test in Perth, December 1970.

Above: Paul Sheehan (Australia) is run out by England fielder Basil D'Oliveira and wicketkeeper Alan Knott for 2 runs in the second Test at Perth, December 1970. Australia went on to make 440 runs in the first innings, with the match finishing in a draw.

Above: Australia's bowler Graham McKenzie walks from the field after capturing four wickets in front of his home crowd against England in the second Test, Perth, in December 1970.

Right: Rival captains Bill Lawry (Australia) and Ray Illingworth (England) toss a coin for a Test match that never was. Owing to heavy rain in Melbourne, the third Test was abandoned without a single ball being played, 6 January 1971.

Left: England skipper Ray Illingworth turns around in time to see his stumps shatter from a delivery from John Gleeson in the fourth Test, in Sydney, in January 1971.

Above: Keith Stackpole (Australia) is caught by Lever of the bowling of Snow for 30, in the fourth Test in Sydney.

Above: Australia wicketkeeper Rod Marsh holds the ball aloft after appealing for a catch behind from England opener Geoff Boycott in the fourth Test. The appeal was turned down by umpire Tom Brooks and Boycott went on to make 77 runs in the first innings. England went on to win a controversial Test by 299 runs.

Left: England's Alan Knott is run out as he desperately lunges for the crease by opposing wicketkeeper Rod Marsh in the fourth Test.

Left: Ray Illingworth and John Snow celebrate England's Test win, following their fourth Test win in Sydney.

Left: England captain Ray Illingworth with his counterpart, Aussie captain Bill Lawry, after the tourists took a 1-0 lead with a fourth Test win at the SCG, January 1971. Lawry made a gallant 60 not out in his attempt to save the match.

Above: Greg Chappell (Australia) is caught by John Edrich (England) off the bowling of Bob Willis in the fifth Test at the MCG. Chappell scored only 3 runs, but Australia later declared their innings after scoring 9-493.

Left: A 'hair-raising' incident in the tour match between the MCC and Perth, February 1971. In the first ball of the match, young Perth bowler Dennis Lillee dislodges Geoff Boycott's cap – with potentially disastrous results.

Below: Australian spin bowler Terry Jenner collapses after being struck by a John Snow bouncer (left) in the final Test of the 1970-71 Ashes series in Sydney, February 1971. Following this incident, SCG spectators threw beer cans on to the pitch before England captain Ray Illingworth led his team from the field.

Above: England Opener Geoff Boycott is caught by Ian Redpath at short square leg off the bowling of Alan Thomson during the drawn fifth Test at the MCG.

Above: Geoff Boycott gets the message that it is time he left the crease, from Australians Ashley Mallett and Greg Chappell after being run-out for 58 in England's first innings against Australia in the sixth Test at Adelaide. The England opener refused to walk to the pavilion and threw his bat to the ground. When he eventually returned he got roundly jeered from the Australian crowd.

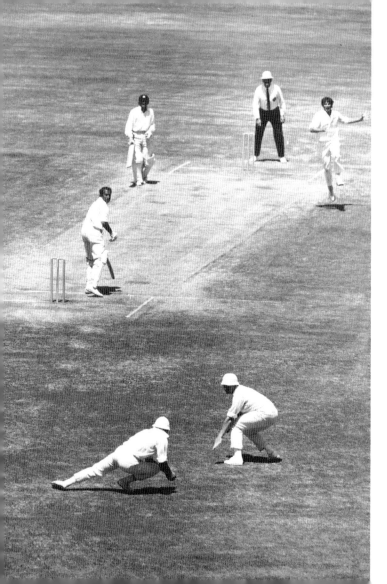

Left: Basil D'Oliveira is out for 47, caught by Australia's captain Ian Chappell off the bowling of Dennis Lillee in the seventh Test in Sydney. England secured the Ashes when it gained a comfortable win over Australia in the final Test of the series.

Right: England fast bowler John Snow cannons into the SCG boundary fence during the controversial Seventh Ashes Test, breaking his wrist.

Above: England bowler John Snow is grabbed by an irate fan at the SCG in the controversial seventh Test of the 1970-71 Ashes series in Australia. Snow had felled Australia batsman Terry Jenner the previous over, firing up the parochial Sydney crowd. As a result of the incident, England captain Ray Illingworth took his team from the field, before common sense prevailed and the Test resumed.

Above: The Pakistan cricket team arrive in London for their tour of England in April 1971. Tour captain Intikhab Alam (back left) with team members on arrival of their London Hotel.

Left: Pakistan cricketer Aftab Gul at batting practise in the nets at Lord's.

Above: Through the gateway into Lord's Cricket Ground, the Pakistan team prepare to practice for their opening tour match against Worcestershire in 1971.

Left: Zaheer Abbas (Pakistan) is out caught first ball by Brian Luckhurst off the bowling of Ray Illingworth, third Test at Headingley.

Above: Queen Elizabeth II is introduced to the Pakistan team by Intikhab Alam before the start of play on day four of the second Test between England and Pakistan at Lord's.

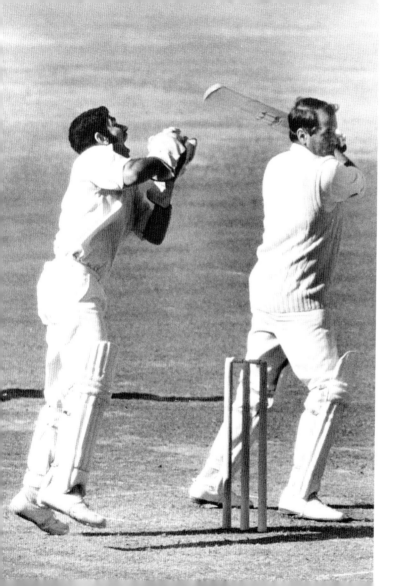

Left: Basil D'Oliveira v Pakistan, 1971.

Right: Pakistan supporters invade the pitch to congratulate Wasim Bari as the visitors took a first innings lead against England in the third Test at Headingley. England ultimately won the match by 25 runs to take the three-Test series 1-0 (2 drawn).

Above: John Edrich (England) is out caught by Wasim Birri (Pakistan wicketkeeper) bowled Asif Masood for 2 on the first day of the third Test between England and Pakistan at Headingley, 8 July 1971. England won an exciting match by 25 runs.

Right: First Test between England and India at Lord's on 26 July 1971. John Edrich turns Bishan Bedi for a quick single on the fourth day of the match, which finished in a draw.

Above: The first Test between England
and India at Lord's. Alan Knot is out caught
Wadekar bowled Venkataraghavan for 67 on
the first day of the match.

Right: Atul Mankad (India) is caught by England wicketkeeper Alan Knott off the bowling of John Snow on the final day of the Test at Lord's.

Below: World XI captain Garry Sobers disguises his bowling hand as he runs to the crease at the Brisbane practice nets in anticipation of the series against Australia in the summer of 1971-72.

Right: Garry Sobers bowling for The Rest of the World against Australia, 1972 ... and he could bat a bit too. In the match at the MCG in January 1972, Sobers hits a six off the bowling of Kerry O'Keefe on his way to a magnificent 254 runs. His innings turned the match on its head, with Australia seemingly in control. The Rest of the World won by 96 runs to level the series at 1-1.

Left: Ray Illingworth is out lbw off Ashley Mallet for 1 on the second day of the match between the MCC and Australia at Lord's, May 1972.

Above: England captain Ray Illingworth drops a catch from Doug Walters (Australia) off the bowling of Geoff Arnold on the third day's play of the first Test at Old Trafford.

Also pictured (from left) are Tony Greig, Brian Luckhurst and keeper Alan Knott.

Left: Keith Stackpole (Australia) takes a catch on tour in England in 1972.

Right: Australia's Bruce Francis is out for 6, lbw to England's John Snow, in the second innings of the First Ashes Test at Old Trafford.

Left: Australia captain Ian Chappell is caught by Alan Knott, bowled John Snow, in the first Test at Old Trafford. England won the Test by 89 runs to take an early lead in the series.

Above: England batsman Mike Denness late cuts John Inverarity for three runs in the second Test at Lord's.

Left: Australia opener Bruce Francis is bowled for a duck by John Snow in the second Test between Australia and England at Lord's.

Above: Australia's star bowler of the 1972 Ashes series, Bob Massie, who captured 23 wickets at just 17.78.

Above: Australian pace bowler Bob Massie (second from left) leaps in the air as wicketkeeper Rod Marsh (right) takes the catch to dismiss England batsman Norm Gifford for 3 runs in the second day's play of the second Test at Lord's. Massie took an incredible 8 wickets in each innings of the match to set up Australia's 8 wicket victory.

Left: Doug Walters (Australia) is out for 2, caught by Peter Parfitt (right) off the bowling of John Snow on the first day of the third Test between Australia and England at Trent Bridge. Australia made 315 runs in the first innings, and 324 in the second, but the match finished in a draw.

Right: England opener Brian Luckhurst is out lbw for 23 to Dennis Lillee on the second day of the third Test at Trent Bridge. The match finished in a draw.

Right: Australian captain Ian Chappell lets a ball pass from England fast bowler John Snow during the fourth Test at Headingley. Australia struggled to make 146 runs in the first innings, resulting in a heavy defeat in the match. Hero for England was Derek Underwood, who took 4-37 and 6-45 as Australia failed in both innings to come to terms with the wicket.

Left: Australian batsman Doug Walters is out, caught by Peter Parfitt off the bowling of Derek Underwood, for 3 runs in the Fourth Ashes Test at Headingley.

Left: Rod Marsh (Australia) is out, caught by Alan Knott bowled Derek Underwood, for 1 in the fourth Tests at Headingley.

Above: Basil D'Oliveira in action against the bowling of Keith Stackpole on the final day of the third Test at Trent Bridge. D'Oliveira went on to score 50 not out with the match finishing in a draw.

Right: Australia batsman Keith Stackpole continues running to the dressing room after being given out lbw off the bowling of Derek Underwood, for 28, in the fourth Test at Headingley.

Right: Ross Edwards (Australia) is out lbw to England's Tony Grieg during Australia's second innings on the final day of the fifth Test at The Oval. Alan Knott and Peter Parfitt (England) are also pictured.

Left: Tony Greig (England) hits bowler Bob Massie (Australia) out to leg in the fifth Test at The Oval.

Left: Greig caught Marsh bowled Lillee. England's Tony Greig was out for 29 runs in the second last day of the fifth Test match of the series, played at The Oval.

Right: England wicketkeeper Alan Knott dives to make a fine stop from Ian Chappell (Australia) off the bowling of Tony Greig in the second ODI at Old Trafford. Australia won by 5 wickets with 21 balls remaining.

Above: MCC Skipper Tony Lewis (left) with team-mate Alan Knott at London's Heathrow Airport on 29 November 1972 before leaving with the rest of his team for their four month tour of India, Pakistan and Ceylon (Sri Lanka).

Right: Australian batsmen Rod Marsh (right) and Paul Sheahan (centre), hastily followed by England's Peter Parfitt (right rear), John Edrich (centre rear), wicketkeeper Alan Knott (left, with pads and cap) and Bob Willis (left), flee the pitch at The Oval as young fans invade the playing area after Australia had won the match to draw the Ashes series 2-all.

Left: The MCC team to India, Ceylon (Sri Lanka) and Pakistan, 1972-73.

Above: India bowler Erapalli Prasanna.

Left and above: Australia fast bowler Jeff Thomson was no slouch with the bat either.

Right: Alvin Kallicharran takes on the England bowling in the first Test at The Oval, July 1973. Kallicharran scored 80 in both innings as the West Indies won by 158 runs.

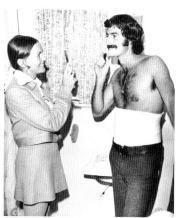

Left: South Africa batsman Barry Richards in 1973.

Above: Dennis Lillee, pictured with wife Helen, recovering from three stress fractures in his back, May 1973. After being injured on the West Indies tour and being placed in a plaster cast, Lillee couldn't put on his shoes and socks at the time. Following a gradual recovery, the champion Australian bowler returned to the game.

Right: West Indies captain Clive Lloyd, 1973.

Above: England fast bowler Alan Ward, who made a welcome return to Test cricket against the West Indies in 1973.

Right: Lord's Cricket Ground in London, the home of cricket, 1974.

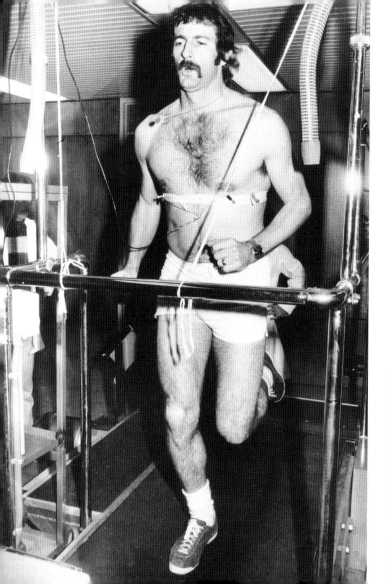

Left: In the biggest gamble of his career, Dennis Lillee trained throughout 1974 to resume his cricket career.

Below: Australian players Garry Gilmour (left) and Rod Marsh (right) play cards as captain Ian Chappell looks on after the third day of the second Test against New Zealand at the SCG, January 1974. This match ended in a draw, after Australia had won the first Test in Melbourne by an innings and 25 runs. Australia were lucky to escape with a draw, being set 456 for a win, they finished day 4 at 2-30. With heavy rain falling stumps were drawn early and on day 5 there was no play possible.

Right: Zaheer Abbas, continuing on his century at The Oval in the final Test match against Pakistan, August 1974, went on to make 240 against England. The Test ended in a draw after Pakistan declared their innings closed at 7 for 600, England replied all out for 545 before Pakistan finished at 4-94 in their second innings.

Left: Doug Walters hits out against Tony Greig in the third Test against the MCC, in Melbourne. Greig would take his wicket in both innings in the only drawn Test of the series. Match scores were: England 242 and 244, Australia 241 and 8-238.

Above: The England team is all smiles in the MCG dressing room after winning the sixth and final Test of the 1974-75 Ashes series by an innings and 4 runs ... but Australia won the series, 4-1, off the back of some brutal fast bowling by Dennis Lillee and Jeff Thomson.

Left: Mike Denness (England) is caught by Greg Chappell off the bowling of Max Walker after scoring 3 during the first innings of the first Test at Edgbaston, Birmingham, 1975. Denness' wicket was one of five taken by swing-bowler Max Walker, while fast-bowler Dennis Lillee captured the other five.

Above: Essex batsman Keith Fletcher takes a run in June 1975. The veteran batsman played Test cricket from 1968 to 1982. He played in 59 Tests and scored 3272 runs at an average of 39.9, hit seven centuries with a high score of 216 against New Zealand at Auckland in 1975.

Left: The umpire confirms the appeal by Dennis Lillee for lbw against John Snow on the third day of the first Test at Edgbaston, July 1975. England was all out for 101, in reply to Australia's first innings total of 359, and went on to lose the Test by an innings and 85 runs.

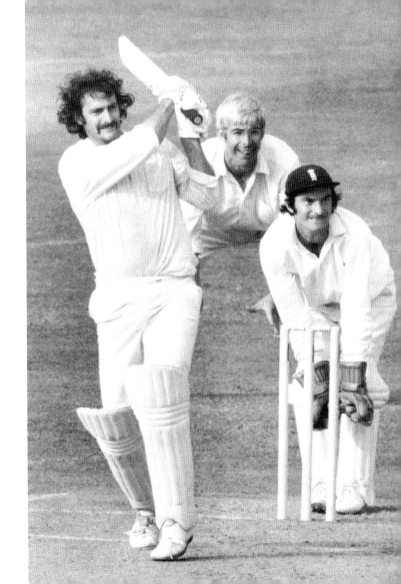

Right: Australian tailender Dennis Lillee scoring a spectacular 73 runs (not out) at Lord's in the second Test. Lillee's innings kept Australia in the contest, rescuing the innings from a perilous 7-81 to a more respectful 268 all out in reply to England's first innings of 315 (after they had been 4-49 at one stage). The match would end in a draw, with England totalling 7 (dec)-436 in their second innings and Australia 3-329 when stumps were drawn on the fifth day.

Left: Australian and England cricket captains Ian Chappell (left) and Tony Greig examine the third Test wicket at Headingley on 19 August 1975, after the pitch was sabotaged by 'Free George Davis' demonstrators. An East London cab driver, Davis had been sentenced to 20 years for armed robbery, but the case had caused wide-spread protest in London. The Test match was later abandoned.

Left: Australia captain Ian Chappell during the 1975 Ashes series in England. In total he would score 429 runs in this series at an average of 71.5, being dismissed six times.

Right: Australia's Ian Chappell sweeps Tony Greig for four as Graham Gooch (left) and wicketkeeper Alan Knott look on during the fourth day's play of the second Test at Lord's, August 1975. Chappell top-scored with 86 as Australia tried to chase down England's lead. The match finished in a draw.

Right: Alan Knott hits out against the Australian team at The Oval, September 1975. Knott's fighting 64 kept England in the match after England trailed by 341 runs on the first innings.

Left: Master batsman Viv Richards avoids a thunderbolt from bowler Dennis Lillee as Rod Marsh dives across to field the ball, Adelaide, January 1976. Richards scored 101 in the second innings of the fifth Test but could not stave off a heavy 190 loss to the Australian team. A very strong Australian side would go on and win the series 5-1, against a powerful (on paper) West Indies side.

Left: This unique photo was taken outside Buckingham Palace at a reception given by The Queen, H.R.H. Prince Philip and H.R.H. Prince Charles for members of the eight teams competing in the 1975 World Series Prudential Cup. The teams were from: Australia, England, East Africa, India, New Zealand, Pakistan, Sri Lanka and West Indies.

Left and above: Feared West Indies fast
bowler Andy Roberts. A brilliant and deadly
accurate fast-bowler, Roberts would capture
202 wickets during his 47 Test career from
1974-1983, at an average of 25.61.

Below: The laidback Lance Gibbs, resting on the boundary during the Test match against Australia in Sydney, 1976.

Right: Veteran West Indies spinner Lance Gibbs is close to tears after receiving a special trophy to mark his breaking of the world record for Test wickets, February 1976.

Right: England versus West Indies. England keeper Alan Knott plays an Andy Roberts bouncer at Headingley in the fourth Test on 12 June 1976. Set 552 runs for victory, England was all out for 126 runs.

Below: West Indies spin bowler Lance Gibbs (centre) is congratulated by teammates Derek Murray (left) and manager Wes Hall after he had equalled the world record for Test wickets (held with England's Fred Truman) in the Test in Adelaide on 27 January 1976. Gibbs would retire at the conclusion of this series after the Melbourne Test in February. His final record would read 79 Tests, 309 wickets at an average of 29.09.

Above: Australian wicketkeeper Rod Marsh. The veteran keeper, nicknamed 'Iron Gloves', is not celebrating catching ten wickets in a Test, but showing his bent and damaged fingers after a career behind the stumps.

Right: Marsh batting with his customary dash on the earlier tour to England.

Left: Tony Greig ducks an Andy Roberts bouncer on the second day of the fourth Test between England and the West Indies at Headingley on June 1976. The West Indies won the Test by 55 runs with Roberts taking three wickets in each innings.

Left: Tony Greig bowling for England XI against The Rest at Bristol, in May 1976. England XI won the three day match by 127 runs.

Below: West Indies 'super batsman' Viv Richard goes after the bowling of Derek Underwood in the fifth Test at The Oval in August 1976. Richards scored 291 runs in West Indies first innings total of 687 runs. After the opening two Tests were drawn the Windies won the remaining Tests to record a resounding 3-0 series win.

Right: The famous MCG scoreboard during the historic Centenary Test in Melbourne, March 1977. Over five days full of action, the Centenary Test didn't disappoint, as Australia won by 45 runs, amid a flurry of action, and great individual performances. Batting first Australia were dismissed cheaply for 138 and looked in a great deal of trouble. However in reply England were torn apart by the great Dennis Lillee (6-26) to be all out for 95. By the close of day two Australia were 3-104 in their second innings and the Test looked destined for an early finish with Australia in complete control. Australia would finally declare their innings closed at 9-419 on day four, with a seemingly insurmountable lead of 462. There had been heroics galore in this innings as David Hookes belted England bowler Tony Greig to all part of the MCG, hitting five successive boundaries in one over on his way to 56, wicketkeeper Rodney Marsh scored 110 not out and a bandaged Rick McCosker batted for 85 minutes to score 25 runs with a broken jaw, courtesy of a Bob Willis bounce in the first innings. Chasing 463 for victory, England's reply was brilliant, falling tantalisingly short of victory, all out for 417. Derek Randall batted superbly for 174 and that man Lillee, was again the hero for Australia, taking 5 for 139.

Left: Members of the Australian team in England, June 1977. From left (behind) Rod Marsh and Dennis Lillee, with tour captain Greg Chappell in front.

Right: Wickets tumbled the second day of the fifth Test at The Oval in August 1977 when England started their innings against Australia, after the opening day was washed out. Geoff Boycott is caught on 39 runs by Rick McCosker off the bowling of Max Walker. While this Test was drawn, England convincingly won the series, with victories in the second, third and fourth Tests, by 3-0.

Above: On left Mike Brearley is dismissed as Robinson at short leg, takes a catch to dismiss the England captain for 49 off the bowling of O'Keefe. Robinson had made several previous attempts to catch Brearley from this position ***(see photo right)***.

Left: The classic bowling action of Dennis Lillee. After he came back from a crippling back injury, Lillee had to adjust his pace and delivery but he was just as effective.

Below: Dennis Lillee, cricket superstar.

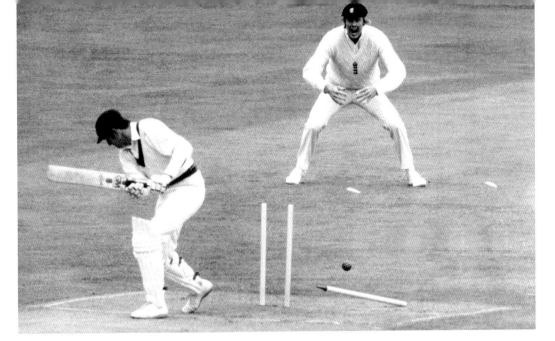

Above: England v Australia Jubilee Test match, 16-21 June 1977, in honour of Queen Elizabeth's 25 years as monarch. Rick McCosker (Australia) is bowled by Chris Old for 23 runs at Lord's.

Left: The MCC touring team assembles at London's Heathrow airport in November 1977 for the tour of New Zealand. Pictured from left are Geoff Boycroft (vice-captain), Ken Barrington (manager) and Mike Brearley (captain).

Left: Australian bowler Max 'Tangles' Walker. A fine right-arm fast medium bowler for Australia, he played 34 Tests from 1973 until 1977 and captured 138 wickets at 27.47

Above: England Test cricketers at Lord's before leaving on their tour of Australia, October 1978. Pictured from left, players Bob Willis, Derek Randall, Mike Hendrick, David Gower and the injured Ian Botham prepare for the 25 match tour of Australia with a game of table cricket.

Above: After dismissing Australia in the third Test at the MCG in December 1978, England was soon in trouble as Rodney Hogg clean bowls Geoff Boycott for 1 run at the opening of the visitors' innings. England captain Mike Brearley, at the non-batting end, saw his side lose the match by 103 runs, but ultimately go on to regain the Ashes.

Right: Graham Gooch batting at Lord's, 21 July 1979, in the final of the Benson and Hedges Cup between Essex and Surrey. Gooch (Essex) drives a ball for two against the bowling of Jackman (Surrey) on his way to making 120 runs.

Below: Brisbane, Australia, December 1978. England's John Lever pours champagne on the head of batsman Derek Randall, man of the match, after England won the first cricket Test of the 1978-79 Ashes series. With scores of 75 and 74 not out, he was top-scorer for England in both innings of the Brisbane Test.

Above: The Australian Test team, without its
'Super Test' players, pictured before taking
on England in Sydney, January 1979.

Left: Australian captain Graham Yallop and bowler of the series, Rodney Hogg (left) in Sydney after the humiliating 5-1 series loss to England, 1978-79.

Above: England captain Mike Brearley celebrates England's staggering win over Australia in the fourth Test in Sydney to regain the Ashes. Australia were in complete control and heading toward victory, before being dismissed for 111 in their second innings. Brearley toasted his team's 93 run victory with a cool beer with players (from left) Miller, Willis and Hendrick, January 1979.

Below: The West Indies training in Australia in the summer of 1979-80 ... the new champions of world cricket.

Above: West Indies captain Clive Lloyd. A brilliant batsman, captain, and in his early days a lightning fast fieldsman, Clive Lloyd captained the Windies masterly through their golden era of the 1970s and 80s. In total he played 110 Tests from 1966 until 1985, totalled 7515 runs at 46.67, scoring 19 centuries and 39 fifties, with a high score of 242 against India in 1975 at Mumbai.

Right: West Indies batsman Viv Richards hooks South Australian bowler Wayne Prior for six in the tour match in Australia, November 1979.

Left: Cricket's top bats challenge for international titles, September 1979. Eight of the world's top batsmen at The Oval, London, in preparation for the Courage International Batsmen of the Year competition. (From left) Gordon Greenidge (West Indies), Zaheer Abbas (Pakistan), Asif Iqbal (Pakistan), Barry Richards (South Africa), Ian Chappell (Australia), David Gower (England), Graham Gooch (England) and Clive Lloyd (West Indies).

This book is dedicated to my wonderful children, Lara and Andrew.

First published in 2015 by New Holland Publishers Pty Ltd
This edition published in 2018 by New Holland Publishers
London • Sydney • Auckland

131–151 Great Titchfield Street, London WIW 5BB, United Kingdom
1/66 Gibbes Street, Chatswood, NSW 2067, Australia
5/39 Woodside Ave, Northcote, Auckland 0627, New Zealand

newhollandpublishers.com

A record of this book is held at the British Library and the National Library of Australia.

ISBN: 9781760790158

Group Managing Director: Fiona Schultz
Publisher: Alan Whiticker
Designer: Andrew Davies
Production Director: James Mills-Hicks
Printer: Toppan Leefung Printing Limited

10 9 8 7 6 5 4 3 2 1

Keep up with New Holland Publishers on Facebook
facebook.com/NewHollandPublishers